THE BOOK OF
Baby Love

THE BOOK OF
Baby Love

*Remembrances on Becoming a Parent from
Madonna, Jacqueline Kennedy Onassis,
Bill Cosby, Rosie O'Donnell, Celine Dion,
and More Than 100 Others*

Edited by Edward Hoffman, Ph.D.

CITADEL PRESS
Kensington Publishing Corp.
www.kensingtonbooks.com

CITADEL PRESS books are published by

Kensington Publishing Corp.
850 Third Avenue
New York, NY 10022

All Kensington titles, imprints, and distributed lines are available at special quantity discounts for bulk purchases for sales promotions, premiums, fund raising, educational, or institutional use. Special book excerpts or customized printings can also be created to fit specific needs. For details, write or phone the office of the Kensington special sales manager: Kensington Publishing Corp., 850 Third Avenue, New York, NY 10022, attn: Special Sales Department, phone 1-800-221-2647.

CITADEL PRESS and the Citadel logo are Reg. U.S. Pat. & TM Off.

First printing: October 2003

10 9 8 7 6 5 4 3 2 1

Printed in the United States of America

Library of Congress Control Number: 2003103853

ISBN 0-8065-2388-3

To Aaron and Jeremy, both beautiful babies

Contents

Acknowledgments, *xiii*
Preface, *xv*

Acquiring Maternal Wisdom   *Sally Field, 1*
Admiring Your Baby   *Isaac Asimov, 3*   /   *Bill Cosby, 4*   /
   Mary Gordon, 5
All Babies Are Unique   *Doris Lessing, 7*   /   *Kuniko Muramoto, 9*   /
   Marcella Bakur Weiner, 10
Allowing Toddlers to Decide   *Kitty Dukakis, 13*
Announcing a Baby's Birth   *Virginia Woolf, 15*
Announcing Fatherhood   *Charles Dickens, 16*   /   *Sigmund Freud, 17*   /
   Dylan Thomas, 18   /   *William Butler Yeats, 19*
Announcing Motherhood   *Abigail Alcott, 21*
Attending Childbirth Class   *Dave Barry, 23*
Attentive Mothering   *Vanessa Williams, 25*
Babies Are a Tourist Attraction   *Paul Reiser, 27*
Babies Are Wise   *Ralph Waldo Emerson, 29*

Becoming a Father   *Tim Allen, 31   /   George Harrison, 32   /
    Don Imus, 34*

Becoming a Grandfather   *Ralph Waldo Emerson, 37*

Becoming a Grandmother   *Lauren Bacall, 38   /   Judy Collins, 40   /
    Tipper Gore, 41*

Becoming a Teenage Mother   *Aretha Franklin, 43*

Becoming an Adoptive Parent   *Diane Engle, 46   /   Mia Farrow, 47   /
    Henry Fonda, 49   /   Jacqueline Mitchard, 51   /   Rosie O'Donnell, 53   /
    Barbara Walters, 56*

Being a Celebrity Dad   *Will Smith, 58*

Being a Celebrity Mom   *Gillian Anderson, 60   /   Meryl Streep, 61*

Building Your Child's Character   *Abigail Adams, 63   /   Katie Couric, 64*

Choosing Parenthood   *Benjamin Spock, 66*

Congratulating a New Father   *John Adams, 68*

Coping with a Prolonged Pregnancy   *Hunter Tylo, 70*

Coping with Medical Circumcision   *Kathie Lee Gifford, 73*

Coping with Stubborn Tots   *Faith Hill, 76*

Cutting the Umbilical Cord   *Kevin Sorbo, 78*

Deciding to Be a Mother   *Sigourney Weaver, 80   /   Debra Winger, 81*

Displaying Fatherly Affection   *Kirk Douglas, 83*

Enjoying Fatherhood   *Theodore Roosevelt, 85   /   Jerry Seinfeld, 86   /
    John Travolta, 87   /   Robin Williams, 89*

Enjoying Motherhood   *Cindy Crawford, 92   /   Namjo Kim, 93   /
    Kelly Ripa, 95*

CONTENTS

Enjoying Pregnancy *Rosalynn Carter, 98 / Cristina Garcia, 99 /
   Barbra Streisand, 100 / Gloria Vanderbilt, 102*

Experiencing Labor *Roseanne, 104 / Cher, 105 / Elizabeth Barrett
   Browning, 108 / Agatha Christie, 109 / Erica Jong, 111 /
   Grace Slick, 112 / Barbra Streisand, 114*

Expressing Fatherly Affection *Kevin Costner, 116*

Expressing Fatherly Pride *Bronson Alcott, 118*

Fatherhood Is a Sacred Bond *Paul Palnik, 120*

Fostering Creativity *Jacqueline Kennedy Onassis, 122*

Gaining Identical Twins *Michael J. Fox, 124*

Gaining Inspiration from Your Baby *Martin Luther King Jr., 127*

Getting Grandmotherly Help *Hank Aaron, 129*

Getting to Know Your Newborn *Maya Angelou, 131*

Getting Toys for Your Child *Mary Todd Lincoln, 134*

Giving Birth to Twins *Madeleine Albright, 136 / Jane Seymour, 138 /
   Cybill Shepherd, 140 / Margaret Thatcher, 142*

Help from the Baby's Siblings *Katharine Graham, 145*

Honoring your Roots *Roxanne Swentzell, 147*

Journaling Your Baby's Birth *Bronson Alcott, 149 /
   Ralph Waldo Emerson, 150*

Keeping Memories Alive *Alicia Ostriker, 151*

Learning the Importance of Faith *Jane Seymour, 153*

Learning to Be a Mother *Eleanor Roosevelt, 155*

Marveling at Your Baby *Samuel Coleridge, 157*

Meeting Your Newborn   *Rebekah Baines Johnson, 159   /
      Sophia Loren, 161*
Motherhood Is a Sacred Bond   *Linda Hogan, 163*
Motherhood Makes You Grow   *Helen Caldicott, 165   /
      Hillary Rodham Clinton, 166   /   Jamie Lee Curtis, 168   /
      Rita Dove, 169   /   Nicole Kidman, 170   /   Reese Witherspoon, 171*
Nurturing a Baby with Disabilities   *Laura San Giacomo, 173   /
      Kelly Preston, 175*
Nurturing a Sick Baby   *Grandma Moses (Anna Mary Robertson), 177*
Opening to Parenthood   *Menachem Schneerson, 179*
Planning for the Birth   *Lucille Ball, 181*
Praying to Have a Child   *Hannah of the Bible, 183   /   LaVera Draisin, 184*
Preparing a Toddler's Birthday Party   *Camryn Manheim, 188*
Raising a Community Baby   *Andrew Young, 190*
Recalling a Pensive Baby   *Mark Twain, 192*
Recalling a Sister's Birth   *Myra Gardner Pierce, 194*
Recalling a Stressful Birth   *Melanie Griffith and Antonio Banderas, 197*
Receiving News of Fatherhood   *Colin Powell, 199*
Rejoicing After the Birth   *Elie Wiesel, 201*
Reminiscing About Childhood   *Bruce Willis, 203*
Respecting Children's Imagination   *Steven Spielberg, 205*
Respecting Your Child's Growth   *Betty Ford, 207   /   Liv Ullmann, 208*
Seeing a Stressful Birth   *Lance Armstrong, 210*
Seeing Babies Mystically   *Bronson Alcott, 212*

CONTENTS

Seeing Children's Joy   *William Blake, 213*

Sharing News About Your Baby   *Lidian Emerson, 216*

Showing Sensitivity to Your Child   *J.K. Rowling, 218*

Surprised by Your Newborn   *Catherine Zeta-Jones, 221*

Talking with Your Child   *Mel Gibson, 223   /   Denzel Washington, 224*

Teaching Love for Reading   *Laura Bush, 227*

Thinking About Fatherhood   *Harrison Ford, 229   /   Bill Gates, 230   /
    Tom Hanks, 232   /   Sylvester Stallone, 233*

Thinking About Motherhood   *Annette Bening, 235   /   Celine Dion, 236   /
    Jodie Foster, 237   /   Diane Keaton, 239   /   Madonna (Ciccone), 240   /
    Michelle Pfeiffer, 242   /   Meg Ryan, 243   /   Maria Shriver, 245   /
    Uma Thurman, 246*

Witnessing the Birth   *Andrea Bocelli, 249   /   Michael Caine, 251   /
    John Denver, 253   /   Frank McCourt, 255   /   Christopher Reeve, 257   /
    Isaac Stern, 259   /   Harry Truman, 260   /   Peter Ustinov, 262*

Working During Pregnancy   *Diana Ross, 264*

Writing to a Baby Nephew   *John F. Kennedy, 266*

Writing to Your Baby   *Richard Harding Davis, 268   /   Mark Twain, 269*

Sources, *271*

Acknowledgments

This book would scarcely have been possible without the valuable help of many people. The enthusiasm of my agent, Alice Fried Martell, was instrumental in bringing this project to the attention of editor Bob Shuman, whose literary judgment and organizational skills are much appreciated. For their encouragement and conceptual contributions on this anthology's theme, I'm much indebted to Fannie Cheng, Eric Freedman, Dr. Ted Mann, Elaine Oshiro, and Paul Palnik. In providing research assistance, Harvey Gitlin, Linda Joyce, and Mia Song again have proven efficient. From start to finish, my family was also a source of lively encouragement and unflagging support.

Preface

It's hard to imagine anything more memorable and joyous than the experience of becoming a parent. Almost invariably, when mothers and fathers are asked to name the most wonderful day of their lives, memories of the birthing surge forward. There's a sweetness about these remembrances—as well as an emotional intensity—that lingers always deep within our consciousness. The sentimental adage is true. No matter the age of our growing—or grown—children, we can't help but see something of their newborn innocence still shining beautifully in their eyes.

As a practicing psychologist for eighteen years and the father of two teenage sons, I know that parenting presents many challenges. From time immemorial this has clearly been the case, and, therefore, it has long comprised the subject of great literature around the world. The Bible, Shakespeare, and countless classic and modern novels alike highlight this potent theme of human life. Additionally, as scientific evidence increasingly shows, each developmental stage from infancy onward carries its own emotional tasks for parent as well as child.

For example, guiding your toddler effectively is very different from guiding your teen. Developmental psychologists now believe that each unfolding stage involves a particular set of sensitivities to youthful feelings and moods, such as curiosity, adventurousness, excitement, elation, boredom, loneliness, and the need for affection. Yet, I'm also convinced that certain qualities are crucial for good parenting at all stages of our youngsters' development: especially trust, patience, perseverance, and faith in our individual intuition, nurturance, and highest values.

Having edited several well-received anthologies related to family life, including *The Book of Fathers' Wisdom* and *The Book of Birthday Wishes*, I was glad to be invited to create one specifically celebrating babies. My earlier, wide-roaming literary excursions into the lives of historically famous men and women had taken me into biographies and memoirs, autobiographies, collected letters, and speeches and interviews, and I looked forward to a similar exploration on this new theme.

More than I even expected, *The Book of Baby Love* has been a delight to produce. In the broadest sense, it has also been marvelously educational: discovering and sharing the early parenting and grandparenting reminiscences of more than 140 leaders internationally in entertainment and the arts, literature and science, and government and public affairs has heightened my awareness of just how wonderful—and ultimately awesome—is the entry of a baby into our adult life. There's no surprise why men and women have always cherished this personal milestone. Whether through biological connection or adoption, it's truly among the greatest gifts and blessings possible to us.

If this book manages in some way to convey this joy, my hopes will have been fulfilled.

THE BOOK OF
Baby Love

Acquiring Maternal Wisdom

Sally Field

The daughter of an actress, California-born Sally Field began her career in lightweight TV sitcoms including *Gidget* and *The Flying Nun*. In 1977, she gained an Emmy for her breakthrough performance as *Sybil*, a young woman with multiple personalities. Two years later, Field won a Best Actress Academy Award and a Cannes Best Actress Prize for her leading role as the labor union organizer *Norma Rae*. Her well-known films include *Places in the Heart* (second Academy Award), *Steel Magnolias, Forrest Gump*, and *Where the Heart Is*. A strong supporter of women's issues, Field traveled to China in the late 1990s to represent Save the Children Forum at the Fourth World Conference on Women.

In an interview for *Good Housekeeping*, Field commented:

[Now that I'm fifty-four, raising a child] is very different. In those days, when I was in my twenties, life seemed like a fog to me. I think that's how it is when you're young and raising a child. You feel overwhelmed, like a wave of responsibility is engulfing you, and there's a loss of self.

I think I have more recognition of what parenting is, more understanding of what my task is. And because my other sons are grown, I have more appreciation of how fast it goes. These years of Sam's adolescence are different. Before that, with his brothers, it seemed like I was going to have to help these horrible, bratty children forever. Now I know it's such a short period of time. And my ability to have an over-vision, to be able to see into the future, is what I can give Sam. Because he can't see any farther than tomorrow afternoon.

Admiring Your Baby

Isaac Asimov

"I must admit that although I don't like children," America's most famous science-fiction author once revealed, "I find little girls far more tolerable than little boys." After the birth of their son, David, when his wife was thirty-five years old and had already experienced fertility problems, Isaac Asimov expected no more children. But less than four years later their daughter, Robyn, was born.

Asimov reminisced, in his third autobiography, published shortly before his death:

> Robyn didn't cry much. She was good natured; she toilet-trained quickly; and in all ways she was satisfactory, except that she did have the habit of (once in a while) drinking her formula and then quietly giving it back to me all over my shirt.
>
> I was delighted [with her] and could never hug and kiss her

enough and tell her how beautiful she was. [My wife] Gertrude objected, thinking perhaps of her own childhood, and said I shouldn't do that. "What if she grows to be a plain woman?" she asked.

I said stoutly, "She won't. And even if she does that, she'll be beautiful in my eyes, and I want her always to know that."

Bill Cosby

An icon in the entertainment world today, Bill Cosby is one of America's most successful TV personalities. The Emmy-winning co-star of the series *I Spy*, narrator of the cartoon *Fat Albert*, and star of the immensely popular *The Cosby Show*, Cosby has also been an active supporter of educational and civic causes. He grew up in an impoverished Philadelphia family and won a football scholarship to Temple University. Unusually, for a highly paid actor of his stature, Cosby returned to college in the 1970s to complete a doctorate in education.

In Cosby's best-selling humor book *Fatherhood*, he wryly observed:

People who have no children say they love them because children are so truthful. Well, I have done extensive fieldwork with [my] five children and can tell you as a scientific fact that the only time they tell the truth is when they are in pain.

A baby, however, sells itself and needs no advertising copy; few people can resist it. There is something about babyness that brings out the softness in people and makes them want to hug and protect this small thing that moves and dribbles and produces what we poetically call poopoo. Even *that* becomes precious, for the arrival of a baby coincides with the departure of our minds.

My wife and I often summoned the grandparents of our first baby and proudly cried, "Look! Poopoo!" A statement like this is the greatest single disproof of evolution I know. Would you like a *second* disproof? Human beings are the only creatures on earth that allow their children to come back home.

A baby overwhelms us with its lovableness; even its smell stirs us more deeply than the smell of pine or baking bread. What is overpowering is simply the fact that a baby is life. It is also a mess, but such an appealing one that we look past the mess to the jewel underneath.

Mary Gordon

Raised in New York City, where she attended parochial school, Mary Gordon is a novelist and essayist who teaches English at Barnard College. The themes of love and duty—filial, maternal, and spousal—are central to her writing. Gordon's novels include *Spending, The Company of Women, Men and Angels, The Other Side, The Rest of Life*, and *Final Payments*, which was nominated for the National Book Critics Circle Award. Her works also include a short story collection, *Temporary Shelter*, and an award-winning memoir, *The Shadow Man*. In Judith Rosenberg's anthology, *A Question of Balance*, Gordon commented:

> My children are the greatest passion of my life and nothing gives me the joy and intensity of feeling and pleasure that they do. . . . As I've moved in the culture of mothers and children, I've been able to observe more mothers and children at close range. . . . I just love those little bodies. I always think they could have a bottle of perfume called Baby Head; it would make a zillion dollars. I love the way they smell and feel, and I love their warmth. I love it when they're sleepy. I really like it when they're a little bit sick—not very sick—but just kind of slowed down, loving and needy.
>
> And I love seeing them run and move. I love seeing the way light falls on them, the way they move through water. Just seeing them move independently and realizing that they really move in the world without you is always exciting.

All Babies are Unique

Doris Lessing

Doris Lessing is among the most venerated British writers today. Born in Iran, she lived on a farm in the country then called Rhodesia with her parents, then quit school at the age of fifteen. Her early jobs included that of nursemaid. Lessing began writing stories while still living in Africa, and published her first novel, *The Grass Is Singing*, in 1950. In this book, Lessing examined white civilization in Africa, her theme in many subsequent works. Lessing's experiences in working-class London after arriving in 1949 are described in *Pursuit of the English*. Her many novels include *The Golden Notebook; The Four-Gated City; Love, Again; The Fifth Child;* and, most recently, *The Sweetest Dream.*

In the autobiographic *Under My Skin*, Lessing recalled her motherhood experience in Rhodesia:

As with the other two babies, I went to the Lady Chancellor Nursing Home. I had no expectations, since I had been wrong twice before, but was in my usual state of pleasurable excitement, invigorated with the need to paint the entire [apartment] or walk twenty miles. This time I did know all this energy announced imminent birth. . . .

No woman who has had more than one baby can subscribe to the doctrine that character is made and not born. When you take an infant in your arms the first time, you are holding what the human being is, its real nature, and whatever else is later done to it—that is the bedrock, the basis, the foundation.

This babe was unlike brave and battling John, unlike sweet and confiding Jean; he was a sleepy but amiable and interested infant. . . .

I was in love with this baby. The mists cleared from my eyes when I sent a photograph to a friend with a letter demanding, "Wasn't this the most beautiful baby she had ever seen?" She sent the photograph back, with the suggestion that I should actually look at it, demanding, "He's just like every other baby. Have you gone completely crazy?" Well, yes, but women do, and it was only for a couple of months.

Kuniko Muramoto

Kuniko Muramoto is a highly respected Japanese psychologist. Director and founder of the Feminine Life Cycle Institute in Osaka, she also teaches at Ritsumeikan University's graduate school. Muramoto, who is married to a psychology professor, has authored several books in Japan on feminine psychology including *Joyful Childbirth* and *Introduction to Women's Studies*. In this essay, Kuniko vividly recalled her two children's differences at birth:

> I gave birth to two children at my parents' house helped by a midwife. This is a very rare case in Japan, but it made possible for me to always be with my newborn babies.
>
> My son, Akira, was a crying baby. He started crying very loudly just after the moment of his birth, and kept crying every evening as if he were furious for his coming into this world. Maybe it was evening colic. I couldn't do anything but just hold Akira and rock him. How hard it was for a mother to accept helplessness toward her baby. I used to whisper to him, "I'm so sorry. I can only be there for you. This is *your* life."
>
> My daughter, Akane, was a happy baby. She seemed to be completely satisfied with her life. I sometimes felt as if she were still in my body when I held her firmly. Her eyes, her mouth,

9

her fists with tiny little nails, and everything stirred up the sense of love in my womb.

Now, as teenagers, my son is gentle but energetic in pursuing his aims. My daughter is rather excitable and a dreamer. Akira is captain of his Judo club and has already gained his black belt. Akane enjoyed her first experience of scuba diving with me at Zamami island and said, "I am the happiest girl in the world."

As a mother, I have learned separation and connection, from both of them. Son, daughter, and mother live their own lives, sometimes celebrating being together.

Marcella Bakur Weiner

A New York City psychologist specializing in couples therapy, Marcella Bakur Weiner is the author of several popular books on relationships including *Repairing Your Marriage After His Affair; Many Paths, One Journey;* and, most recently, *The Book of Love Compatibility*, written jointly with me. As a psychological commentator, Weiner appears regularly on TV shows including *Geraldo* and *Court TV*, and co-hosted her own radio talk-show, *Choices*. Her husband is a practicing psychotherapist. In an essay related to her new book on love compatibility, Weiner reminisced:

With my first-born son, I was the new, fiercely dedicated mother. Following the rules of my soon-to-be profession as psychologist, I was going to not just be the "good-enough mother" of the parenting books, but the best. And so, with his cry piercing the air with high emotional intensity, I, like the tuning fork near the one which is struck, vibrated similarly. He wanted to be fed. I flew into the room to nurse, dropping all activities without flinching.

Prior to speech, when he most assertively pointed his tiny fingers outward, I scurried to present him with object after object until we could both settle on his choice. We were a team, I having concluded that this is what babies are all about. Until two and a half years later, when my second son was born.

"Well," I thought, "I am conditioned. The rest is easy." He cried, I ran. Surprise!

Totally disconnected from the cry, he was scanning the room and looking up at me with a message that clearly stated, "Oh, that cry, let it go. Whatever it was I wanted, forget it, we can wait. Let's just both take it slow." And so, out of mother-love and a sensitivity to his unique needs, I reconditioned myself onto another place.

Babies once, they are now two adults, loving sons and friends, each wrapped in their own skins, their unique differences having

11

grown along with them. As for me, my early life-course in mothering taught me that our personality, created at birth, flowers throughout life.

The ultra-lesson is to love this within ourselves, in the other, and by extension, in all of humanity. Taught to me at the cribside of my sons, it has been a boon to my work as a practicing psychologist and infused my private life with a magic and glory I might otherwise never have suspected.

Allowing Toddlers to Decide

Kitty Dukakis

The former First Lady of Massachussetts, Kitty Dukakis received public scrutiny after her husband Michael Dukakis's unsuccessful presidential bid against George Bush in 1988. Like Betty Ford, she admitted to a long-time struggle with alcoholism and sought appropriate treatment. Since obtaining a social work degree in the early 1990s, Kitty has actively worked with immigrants and refugees, and was appointed by President Clinton to the U.S. Holocaust Commission. She and Michael have several grandchildren.

In her revealing memoir, *Now You Know*, Kitty Dukakis recalled:

> I had been brought up in a certain way by my mother, and I was determined to do things differently with my children. Sound familiar? With my son, the job was a bit easier. Raising a boy was new territory, no precedent had been set, and, once Michael

came into his life, John had a role model. Andrea and Kara presented certain problems.

Unlike me, I wanted my girls to be independent from the start. My dependence on my parents helped propel me into an early marriage because I mistakenly believed marriage would endow me with self-determination. I wanted my children to make their own decisions whenever possible, right from the beginning.

At two years of age, Andrea Dukakis chose her own wardrobe. My mother would come over to the house and go nuts watching her pint-sized granddaughter standing in front of the closet deciding what she would put on for the day.

"How can you let a two-year-old pick out her clothes?" Mother demanded.

"Because I want her to; it's good for her," I answered.

Announcing a Baby's Birth

Virginia Woolf

Virginia Woolf was a major British novelist, critic, and essayist. With acclaimed novels including *Mrs. Dalloway, Night and Day*, and *To the Lighthouse*, Woolf was a pioneer of stream-of-consciousness writing and a founding figure of the twentieth century's modernist literary movement. Born into an affluent London family, she became a leading figure in what came to be known as the "Bloomsbury" group of London's early-twentieth-century cultural avant-garde.

In a December 1918 letter to a friend, Woolf effusively wrote:

Have you heard of Nessa's daughter? She was born on Christmas Day, very successfully, and they both seem to be doing well. Nessa sounds very happy, and says the baby is already perfectly beautiful—with large blue eyes, Greek nose, lovely mouth, and adorable character. She was very pleased it was a daughter, and so am I—As you politely say beauty and talents seem inevitable, considering her aunt.

Announcing Fatherhood

Charles Dickens

As England's most famous writer of the nineteenth century, Charles Dickens enjoyed a huge and appreciative audience. His novels like *Oliver Twist* and *Great Expectations* often vividly depicted children struggling for their place in an indifferent world. Dickens himself had ten children, and their problems consumed his attention throughout his life. In January 1837, he penned these droll words to his illustrator George Cruikshank:

> According to all established forms and ceremonies, I ought to have written on Friday evening last, to duly acquaint and inform Mrs. Cruikshank that Mrs. Dickens had at a quarter past six o'clock P.M. presented me with a son and heir. But as I know you are not ceremonious people, and as we are very much in the same way, I thought I might just as well defer the communica-

tion until I had something else to say: knowing that the importance of such [news] diminishes very materially outside one's own house.

Sigmund Freud

Sigmund Freud, the most influential psychological thinker in history, experienced strained relations with colleagues throughout his life. He was arrogant toward those who disagreed with his tenet that sexuality is the key factor in human personality. In later years, Freud's philosophical writings were marked by an increasingly bitter, cynical view of human nature. But he also had a warm, gentle side.

In October 1887, Freud presented these buoyant words to his mother and sister Minna:

I am terribly tired and have so many letters to write, but the first must go to you. You will have heard already by telegram that we have a little daughter. She weighs nearly seven pounds, which is quite respectable, looks terribly ugly, has been sucking at her right hand from the first moment, seems otherwise to be very good-tempered and behaves as though she really feels at home here.

In spite of her splendid voice, she doesn't cry much, looks very happy, lies snugly in her magnificent carriage and doesn't give any impression of being upset by her great adventure. She is called Mathilde, of course, after Frau Dr. Breuer.

How can one write so much about a creature only five hours old? The fact is that I already love her very much, although I have not yet seen her in the daylight.

Dylan Thomas

"I hold a beast, an angel, and a madman inside of me," declared Dylan Thomas, one of Britain's leading mid-twentieth-century poets. Born in Swansea, Wales, Thomas worked briefly as a full-time journalist before embarking on a freelance literary career. Despite a short life marked by alcoholism and depression, Thomas achieved lasting fame for such prose works as *Adventures in the Skin Trade, Portrait of the Artist as a Young Dog*, and *Quite Early One Morning*. He also published many short stories, wrote film scripts, broadcast stories and talks, and wrote *Under Milkwood*, a radio play for voices.

In March 1939, Thomas sent a friend this exciting news:

This is to tell you with variations what I'm sure you must know by now—that I'm the father of a son named Llewelyn, aged six weeks: a fat, round, bald, loud child with a spread nose and blue saucer eyes.

His full name is Llewelyn Edouard, the last being a concession to Caitlin's French grandfather. But in spite of this, he sounds militantly Welsh, and though this is probably national pride seen through paternal imagination, or vice versa, he looks it too. . . . Oh yes, I'm set in life now—two stone heavier, but not a feather steadier.

William Butler Yeats

"Tread softly because you tread on my dreams," wrote William Butler Yeats, considered one of the greatest English-language poets of the twentieth century. Leader of the Irish Literary Renaissance in the early 1900s, Yeats drew from legend, occultism, and personal mystical experience to fashion a new vision of human existence in the modern world. His works include *The Tower, The Wild Swans at Coole*, and *The Wind Among the Reeds*. In 1922, Yeats became a senator of the Irish Free State after the Anglo-Irish war, and the following year he received the Nobel Prize for literature.

To an old chum in August 1921, Yeats happily confided:

Georgie had a son on August 22nd, as I hope John Butler Yeats told you, and we want you to be a godfather. The other godfather will, I hope, be Lennox Robinson, who has already been godfather to two Czech-Slav children whose names he has forgotten and could never pronounce. They were born on the boat that carried him and the Abbey players to Boston.

I tell you this that you may not shrink from your responsibility. It is Georgie's idea. She is very set on your taking the post.

Both Georgie and the child are well, and the doctor says that he has a "beautiful head." All I can say is that he is better looking than a newborn canary—I had four hatch out in my bedroom a little while ago—and nothing like as good-looking as the same bird when it gets its first feathers.

Announcing Motherhood

Abigail Alcott

Abigail May Alcott, mother of the novelist Louisa May Alcott, was born in Boston, in 1800, the youngest of twelve children. Looking back on her youth, she recalled candidly, "My schooling was much interrupted by ill health, but I danced well and at the dancing school, I had for partners some boys who afterwards became eminent. I did not love study, but books were attractive."

At the age of nineteen, Abigail broadened her education with a private tutor in French, Latin, botany, and history. She first met her future husband, the social reformer and philosopher Henry Amos Alcott, at her brother's (the Reverend Samuel May's) home. It was apparently love at first sight, for in Abigail's view, she had finally met, at age thirty, "the only being whom I ever loved as companionable." They raised four daughters, including Louisa May Alcott, the famed author of *Little Women* and other works.

Twelve days after giving birth to Anna in March 1831, she poured out her joy to Samuel and his wife:

I am so well and happy that I cannot resist any longer to give you some actual demonstration of my strength and enjoyment. My dear Sam and Lu, you have rejoiced with me ere this in the safe birth of my child. My happiness in its existence and the perfection of its person is quite as much as I can well bear.

Had she not lived an hour after the pangs of birth, I should still rejoice that she had been born. The joy of that moment was sufficient compensation for the anguish of thirty-six hours. But she has lived long enough to open all the fountains of my higher and better nature. She has given love to life, and life to love.

Attending Childbirth Class

Dave Barry

Dave Barry, a syndicated columnist for the *Miami Herald*, is widely read for such humorous books as *Dave Barry Slept Here, Claw Your Way to the Top*, and *Dave Barry's Guide to Marriage and/or Sex*. Raised in suburban New York City, he decided on a journalism career, and he first gained wide popularity in the 1980s for his satirical articles on contemporary family life and other topics. In *Dave Barry Is Not Making This Up*, he turned his wit to a facet of contemporary fatherhood:

> We had to go to ten evening childbirth classes at the hospital. Before the classes, the hospital told us, mysteriously, to bring two pillows. This was the first humiliation, because no two of our pillowcases match and many have beer or cranberry-juice stains. It may be possible to walk down the streets of Kuala Lampur with stained, unmatched pillowcases and still feel dignified, but this is not possible in American hospitals. . . .

The class consisted of a sitting in a brightly lit room and openly discussing, among other things, the uterus. Now I can remember a time, in high school, when I would have *killed* for reliable information on the uterus. But having discussed it at length, having seen actual full-color *diagrams*, I must say in all honesty that although I respect it a great deal as an organ, it has lost much of its charm. . . .

We saw lots of pictures. One evening, we saw a movie of a woman we didn't even know having a baby. I am serious. Some women actually let moviemakers film the whole thing. In color. She was from California.

Another time, the instructor announced, in the tone of voice you might use to tell people they had just won free trips to Hawaii, that we were going to see color slides of a caesarian section. The first slides showed a pregnant woman cheerfully entering the hospital. The last slides showed her cheerfully holding a baby. The middle slides showed how they got the baby out of the cheerful woman, but I can't give you a lot of detail here because I had to go out for fifteen or twenty drinks of water. I do remember that at one point our instructor cheerfully observed that there was surprisingly little blood, really. She evidently felt this was a real selling point.

24

Attentive Mothering

Vanessa Williams

Vanessa Williams made history in 1983 by becoming the first African-American woman to be named Miss America. One year later, she was stripped of her crown after nude photos, taken years before, were published by *Penthouse* magazine. However, the controversy was only a minor setback to her career; Williams persevered and has gone on to enjoy considerable success as both an actress and a singer.

Her film credits include *Eraser, Hoodlum, Soul Food*, and *Dance with Me*. She has also starred on Broadway in such plays as *Into the Woods* and *Kiss of the Spider Woman*. Williams's best-known albums, which have earned her nine Grammy nominations, include *The Right Stuff, The Comfort Zone, Sweetest Days*, and *The Greatest Hits: The First Ten Years*. In 1995, Williams recorded the Oscar-winning song "Colors of the Wind" from the Disney movie hit *Pocahontas*.

Married to NBA star Rick Fox in 1999, the two have a daughter named Sasha. In an interview with *Ebony*, Williams said:

I've heard comments about how I can be so calm as a mother, and then they say, "Your kids are really calm and polite." It's the tone you set. I don't scream at them. I don't hit them. I reason with them. I give them boundaries and limits, and they know there are consequences for their actions. That is what makes them the kids they are. Don't humiliate them. Make them feel like individuals, but also that there is certainly a line that you don't cross. And you have to respect me as a mother, and respect your parents and your elders. They learn by example.

[I want my kids to] feel comfortable in their own skin, to feel proud of their heritage, who they are and where they are from. And that they are not afraid to follow what is inside their hearts. . . . I hope they have the courage to go for whatever it is they want.

Babies Are a Tourist Attraction

Paul Reiser

Tenderly known to millions as loving, but very human husband Paul Buchman on the TV show *Mad About You*, New York–born Paul Reiser is also a writer, comedian, and producer. He majored in piano before pursuing an acting career and has enjoyed a longtime friendship with Jerry Seinfeld. Reiser is married to a psychotherapist; his recent humorous books include *Couplehood* and *Babyhood*. In *Babyhood*, Reiser wryly observed:

> A new child in the house is a huge tourist attraction. It's like Disneyland, except there the lines are longer and no one brings casseroles. Everybody has to come, everybody has to see.
>
> And everybody has to *hold* the baby. I remember being naturally protective of our infant son. During those first few days, regulations were firmly established.

 27

"Okay, you have to wash your hands before you handle the baby. You have to remove any sharp objects to be found on your person or clothing. If you've had a cold in the last eighteen months you must sit in the den until spring."

Even though we had been parents for less than forty-eight hours, we felt perfectly justified in giving expert instructions to everyone. Like a newly founded country, we already had our laws, bylaws, and traditions.

"Uh, Mom, that's not how he likes to be held. We always support his neck . . . like this."

"Always?"

"Well, since yesterday."

Boy, nothing endears you to your parents more than telling them how to deal with babies.

"Do you remember me dropping you a lot when *you* were a baby?"

"Um, no, not really, but . . ."

"Did your father drop you a lot, that you recall?"

"No, but you don't . . ."

"So, why don't you calm down and get your wife a sandwich?"

Babies Are Wise

Ralph Waldo Emerson

Children were important to Ralph Waldo Emerson, who ranks among America's greatest philosophers. He inspired numerous writers and thinkers including his close friend Henry David Thoreau, as well as Emily Dickinson, Herman Melvile, and Henry James. Originally trained as a Unitarian minister, Emerson became immensely successful as an independent writer and lecturer. His key themes included self-reliance and creative individuality.

In a journal entry a few days after his first child, Waldo, was born in October 1836, Emerson mused:

It seemed yesterday morn as the snow fell, that the adult looks more sourly than the child at the phenomenon of approaching winter. The child delights in the first snow and sees with it the spruce and hemlock boughs they bring for Christmas with glee.

The man sees it all sourly, expecting the cold days and inconvenient roads and labors of winter.

But the experience of a thousand years has shown him that his faculties are quite equal to master these inconveniences, and despite of them, to get his bread and wisdom. Therefore the child is the wiser of the two.

Becoming a Father

Tim Allen

Tim Allen is best known for starring in the long-running TV hit *Home Improvement*, in which he played a bumbling TV handyman. His recent films include *The Santa Clause, Galaxy Quest, Joe Somebody*, and *Santa Clause 2*; Allen also provided the voice for cartoon character Buzz Lightyear in Disney's computer-generated extravaganzas *Toy Story* and *Toy Story 2*.

Born Timothy Allen Dick, one of ten children, he was mercilessly teased by his peers because of his last name and developed a keen sense of humor to protect himself. Known early in his career for vulgar routines and a prison stint for cocaine dealing, Allen has well transformed himself into an appealing figure for children. In his bestseller *Don't Stand Too Close to a Naked Man*, Allen observed:

> An odd thing about fatherhood is the change in camaraderie with other male parents, especially when your kids are still very

small. You bond, but the adhesion principle is altogether differ-ent from the stereotypical macho posturing about one's fertility and already being able to pay for the kid's college education. That went out long ago, with the eighties. This bond is rife with genuine tenderness, vulnerability, and a little sadness. I don't know why. It just is—maybe because having a kid finally con-nects a man to something he loves unconditionally that, unlike his car or power tools, can actually love him in return.

George Harrison

Celebrated as the "quiet one" of the Fabulous Four Beatles, Harrison wrote such memorable songs as "While My Guitar Gently Weeps," "Here Comes the Sun," and "Something." Born into a working-class Liverpool family during World War II, he began performing rock-and-roll as a teenager. In the fall of 1962, when Harrison was all of eighteen, the Beatles released their first single, which paired the Lennon-McCartney compositions "Love Me Do" and "P.S. I Love You."

After the Beatles broke up, Harrison continued to write and record, and his solo career peaked with such albums as *All Things Must Pass* and *The Concert for Bangladesh*. Featuring songs like "My Sweet Lord," and "What Is Life?" these solidified his reputation for effectively mixing rock and religion. Following a stint as a film producer, Harrison reappeared as one of the Traveling Wilburys, a band that also included Bob Dylan, Roy Orbison, and Tom Petty.

As described by biographer Marc Shapiro in *Behind Sad Eyes*, Harrison's life in the '80s gained renewed excitement with his second marriage, to Olivia Arias, and the birth of their son, Dhani.

The months of Olivia's pregnancy were a time of great joy and contentment for George. Almost daily he would caress his wife and put his hand on her stomach to feel the kick of life inside her. He kept his business commitments to a bare minimum and was never more than a telephone ring away from Olivia. . . .

On August 1, 1978, George, at the advanced age, for fatherhood, of thirty-eight, was a bundle of nervous energy and conflicting emotions as he paced the halls of the Princess Christian Nursing Home in nearby Windsor. Olivia had gone into labor that day and would give birth to a son. True to the couple's collective spiritual and religious leanings, the child was named Dhani, which is Sanskrit for "wealthy."

George's protective nature immediately escalated upon the birth of his son. George instantly ran out and bought a brand-new Rolls Royce, colored blue of course, so that his wife and son would not be bounced around on the ride home from the hospital.

Overcompensation was the order of the day once the happy family returned to Friar Park. George insisted that his son not leave the house, and even those few friends and relations who were allowed to see the baby were not allowed to touch him. Harry, long used to his younger brother's eccentricity, was astonished by George's latest bit of nuttiness.

"I was a bit surprised," Harry recalled laughingly. "I mean, I've got two kids of my own. But it must have been two or three months before he would even let me touch the baby."

Don Imus

John Donald Imus—known simply to his vast listening audience as Imus—is one of America's most popular radio talk show hosts. Growing up in California and Arizona, he was unsuccessful as a rock musician in his early career and showed greater prowess as a disk jockey. Starting in 1971 on WNBC in New York City, his program "Imus in the Morning" gained notoriety for its use of "insult humor," often coarse and controversial; he subsequently suffered several career setbacks owing to alcohol and drug abuse. Now heard on hundreds of stations every day, Imus offers a unique blend of political satire, sports gossip, and, most recently, meandering chitchat about Imus's family and philanthrophic activities for cancer-stricken children who come as visitors to his sprawling New Mexico ranch.

In *Imus, America's Cowboy*, biographer Kathleen Tracy described his experience of starting a new family (after raising four daughters from a first marriage) in his mid-fifties:

> When they first got married, Imus had brushed aside questions about whether he and Deidre would start a family by saying he was already marrying a baby. But in the autumn [that year] Deidre became pregnant and suddenly Imus was facing the prospect of starting a new family at fifty-seven years of age. But Imus chose not to dwell on the age factor. "If you don't know how old you were, how old would you be? So I figure I'd be about forty."
>
> In preparation for the birth of their baby, Imus bought a house in Westport, Connecticut, best known as the home of Martha Stewart, for $4.6 million. . . . The plans included a nursery and a nanny's room.
>
> Then, in July 1998, Frederick Wyatt Imus was born, and Don's life took perhaps the most unexpected turn of all. Don was enthralled with all things Frederick Wyatt, even the birth.
>
> "That was great. I know this is going to sound idiotic, but you actually have to love your wife, but you also have to really like

35

them, because you're right in there, it's war. My wife is great because she's an athlete, so she looked at the pushing like an athletic event. She was great. I was helping her count."

Then Don described the moment when the baby was born. "The child, his head comes out, and I said, 'He's got red hair!' The doctor was saying, 'No, I think that's blood.' Well, there's blood all over the place, but I could see it was red hair. Well, I had red hair fifty years ago. . . ."

"When we had this little red-headed boy, I couldn't stop crying. I don't cry about anything. I couldn't stop crying the first week. I went to work [one morning], left the apartment about four-thirty and was crying on the way to work. I don't know why. This afternoon he slept on my chest for about three hours. There's no way to describe it."

Becoming a Grandfather

Ralph Waldo Emerson

Emerson was a devoted husband and tender father who wrote many letters to his children whenever he was on his frequent speaking tours. In July 1866, the sixty-three-year-old philosopher was at home in Concord when news of his first grandchild arrived. Emerson immediately sent his daughter Edith these sentimental words:

> Happy wife and mother that you are—and not the less surely that the birth of your babe touches this old house and its people and neighbors with unusual joy. I hope the best gifts and graces of his father and mother will combine for this blossom, and highest influences hallow and ripen the firm and perfect fruit. There is nothing in this world so serious as the advent of a child with all his possibilities to parent with good minds and hearts. Fair falls the little boy—he has come among good people. . . . I please myself that his fortunes will be worthy of these great days of his country, that he will not be frivolous, that he will be noble and true, and will know what is sacred.

Becoming a Grandmother

Lauren Bacall

Lauren Bacall was one of Hollywood's leading actresses for several decades. Beautiful, tough-talking, and husky-voiced, she debuted at the age of nineteen, playing opposite Humphrey Bogart in the 1944 movie *To Have and Have Not*. She subsequently married "Bogie," a quarter-century her senior, creating a formidable team both on and off screen. Like Greta Garbo and Marlene Dietrich before her, Bacall was able to play a wide range of roles successfully, from the wealthy, enigmatic Vivian in *The Big Sleep* to the distraught wife in *Written on the Wind*. Married to second husband, actor Jason Robards Jr., for eight years, Bacall returned to the screen in 1974 for *Murder on the Orient Express*.

In her memoir entitled *Now*, the famous actress recalled:

I couldn't believe it. The voice on the other end of the phone said: "Are you ready to be a grandma again?" Sam, it was my

Sam, my baby, telling me [that] he and Suzy were going to have a baby. It was unreal. How did it happen so fast, his growing up? There had been small, imperceptible changes since his wedding almost five years before. At times when he's been frustrated in his work, and I've told him what to do about it or what I thought he should do, he has said, in the gentlest, nicest kind of way, "You have your way of dealing with things and that's fine for you, and I have mine. I'll handle it, but in my own way."

[Within the year, Bacall had the grandchild:]

Two weeks old, and Sam had given him a daily bath. He'd done everything but nurse him. It was so fabulous to see my baby swinging *his* baby in his car seat, handling him with total ease. One night he was holding him, studying him, and shaking his head from side to side. I asked him what he was thinking, and he said, "I can't believe it."

Nor could I. This child of mine, whom I'd spent so much time with alone, watching him from year to year: there I was watching him again, as he held a baby straight out in front of him in his two hands, only it was not a baby—it was *his* baby.

Judy Collins

Judy Collins was a folk-singing icon of the tumultuous '60s, closely linked in public awareness to performers like Bob Dylan; Joan Baez; and Peter, Paul, and Mary. A child prodigy at classical piano, she turned to folk music at the age of fifteen and released her first album, *A Maid of Constant Sorrow*, in 1961, when she was twenty-two. She gained attention quickly for her pure, sensitive sopranic interpretation of traditional British ballads and new tunes like "Turn, Turn, Turn" and "The Times they Are A-Changin'."

In 1967, Collins's first of six gold albums, *Wildflowers*—containing the hit single "Both Sides Now," written by Joni Mitchell—catapulted her to enduring fame. During the Vietnam War era, Collins was associated in the public eye with political and social protest. Yet, she was also uniquely admired for innovative pop music performances, making use of Broadway and orchestral arrangements in such stirring songs as Stephen Sondheim's "Send in the Clowns," or singing "Amazing Grace" a cappella.

Collins continues to perform both traditional and new material before appreciative audiences. In her memoir, *Singing Lessons*, she reminisced:

Once, just after my granddaughter was born, Alyson carried her to see me, at the hotel where I was staying in St. Paul, a tiny girl in a basket, with big blue eyes like her father's, and cherry lips like her mother's, laughing up at me. From the high hills in St. Paul, I could hear the big bell of the cathedral tolling the time, chiming the hours. I felt the murmur of my genes, ancient voices in my blood, the purpose of my life, the completion of my role.

My granddaughter's beautiful face looked up at me. "You can die now, she is carrying your line," the voice of my ancestors whispered. I was shocked to feel the primitive call from my civilized exterior. It is all genetic, all karmic, I thought, all this agony and all this joy.

It was heaven to have a loving relationship with my son now in this time of beauty, work, health, family.

All the things I had always hoped for Clark had come true.

Tipper Gore

Political activist and photographer, Mary Elizabeth Gore is best known as wife of former U.S. Vice President Al Gore. Nicknamed "Tipper" by her mother, she grew up inside the Washington, D.C. Beltway and met her future husband, Al Gore, at a high school graduation dance. In 1970, they were married at Washington National Cathedral, and in the same year she received her degree in psychology from Boston University, later earning a master's degree. An avid pho-

41

tographer, Tipper worked in Nashville for the *Tennessean* until her husband was first elected to Congress in 1976. Several years later, she gained national attention for co-founding the Parents' Musical Resource Center, to promote parental and consumer awareness of lurid content in popular music marketed to children.

During the Clinton administration and after, Tipper Gore has forcefully advocated on behalf of those with mental illness. In a recent interview, she commented about an especially happy milestone in life:

People don't really prepare you for the profound emotional impact of becoming a grandparent. You're very excited and thrilled, the baby is born, you hold him, and you're sort of in shock. There's kind of a backslapping, bumper-sticker version of it, which is great. I'm doing it myself. But what it really does is show you where you are in the cycle of life. It takes time to get used to that and its implications. And it's a wonderful experience to watch your child become transformed as a parent, which doesn't happen just like that. It's a process.

Becoming a Teenage Mother

Aretha Franklin

The acclaimed "Queen of Soul" was born in Memphis and moved as a child with her family to Detroit during World War II. Her father, Clarence LaVaughn (known as C.L.), was a famous minister, and her mother a gospel singer who died when Aretha was only ten years old. As a result, it was C.L. who played the key role in encouraging Aretha's musical talent and vocal education. Guests at his Detroit home included Sam Cooke, B.B. King, Mahalia Jackson, Lou Rawls, and Dinah Washington.

Franklin's first album, recorded in 1960, made no overwhelming success when released for Columbia Records. But after switching to Atlantic Records, her career skyrocketed in the late '60s with such hit singles as "Baby I Love You," "Chain of Fools," "(Sweet Baby) Since You've Been Gone," "Think," and two of her trademark tunes, "(You Make Me Feel Like) A Natural Woman" and "Respect." Franklin again epitomized an era when in 1968 she sang "Precious Lord" at the funeral of slain civil rights leader Dr. Martin Luther King Jr., who had been a close friend of her father.

Accomplishment has continued to follow Franklin, who in 1993 sung at President Bill Clinton's inauguration and in 1999 was awarded the National Medal of Arts by the National Endowment for the Arts. In her memoir, *Aretha*, the famed singer recalled a very different major milestone in her life:

Daddy had been telling me not to associate with the girl down the street, who he felt was too fast for me. Subsequently he noticed my weight gain and told me he was taking me to the doctor. Just as I suspected, I was pregnant.

Some fathers have been known to put their daughters out of their homes, but not my dad. He was not judgmental, narrow, or scolding. He simply talked about the responsibilities of motherhood. He was a realist, and he expected me to face the reality of having a child. The days of spiced ham and Popsicles were over. I was becoming a young adult and a parent all at once.

For a short while, my boyfriend and I would meet in our backyard late at night and discuss the future. For a Detroit minute, we talked about running off to get married. Thank God we didn't, because Daddy would have killed him. My father knew we were far too young to make that kind of commitment. We hardly knew what commitment meant.

In my fifth or sixth month, I dropped out of school. My family supported me in every way. The doctor put me on a special diet because I was gaining too much weight, but the pregnancy went very well. When my baby was born, I had just turned fourteen, not the easiest or best age to begin a family, but a blessing nonetheless. All children are gifts from God; all children are miracles.

I accepted the blessing and named my son Clarence, after my dad. Everyone adored Clarence. He was a beautiful little baby with a beautiful temperament. . . . The love between a mother and a child is forever. This was my baby, I intended to love and care for him, and I did.

Becoming an Adoptive Parent

Diane Engle

Diane Engle is a professional writer whose poetry and essays have appeared in numerous journals in the United States, Canada, and Britain. Her work is also included in an anthology, *The Muse Strikes Back: A Poetic Response by Women to Men*. Originally trained as an attorney, Engle is also an organist and pianist who makes her home in Bellingham, Washington. In an anthology edited by Susan Wadi-Ells entitled *The Adoption Reader*, Engle humorously recounted:

> It is a good many years now since my daughter, Desiree, then age four, burst indignantly through the back door with a doubting—nay, scoffing—friend in tow. "Mommy," Desi demanded, "I'm adopterated, aren't I?"
>
> These many years later, Desi is still fascinated with her status as an adopted child. Yet it is she who snuggled up beside me one

day sometime later and dropped this bombshell. "You aren't my *real* mother, are you?"

I thought, well, little girl, whose diapers I changed from the day you were four-days-old, whose food spitting I lived with for eleven months, whose bone disease and brace I endured, whose smart mouth I have tolerated and to some degree tamed, whose temper tantrums I have ignored, whose independence and emotionalism I have loved and nurtured: What kind of thing is that to say to *me?*

I hugged her. "Desi," I said, "I've lived with you and loved you since you were four days old. There is nothing more real than that."

Mia Farrow

Mia Farrow is the daughter of director John Farrow and actress and Tarzan-girl Maureen O'Sullivan. In 1959, at the age of fourteen, Mia debuted with several small film roles, and on Broadway four years later in the revival of Oscar Wilde's *The Importance of Being Earnest*. In 1968, Mia's performance in *Rosemary's Baby*, directed by Roman Polanski, marked her Hollywood breakthrough. But it was as Woody Allen's muse in such films as *A Midsummer Night's Sex Comedy, Broad-*

way Danny Rose, The Purple Rose of Cairo, and *Zelig* that Farrow became a celebrated actress. Known for her marriages to Frank Sinatra, conductor-composer Andre Previn, and a bitterly ending romance with Woody Allen, Farrow retains a persona of waif-like delicacy and fragility; her recent films include *Coming Soon* and *Purpose*.

Farrow has ten adopted children, one of whom, Indian-born Thaddeus, was stricken with polio, which Farrow herself contracted in 1954. She is active today on behalf of UNICEF's mission to eradicate polio from the world. In her memoir, *What Falls Away*, Mia Farrow recalls her first adoptive experience:

In 1974, we had written to the director of the orphanage in Vietnam, hoping to adopt another child. But then South Vietnam was invaded by the North, and unforgettable images of panic and pandemonium were transmitted around the world. . . .

In rural England, with the daffodils just coming into bloom, I was watching all this on television when a telegram, impossibly, arrived from Saigon saying that a baby girl had been chosen for us and put on the airlift—look for her at Presidio Air Force Base in California. Her identification number was H-2. I phoned through the night trying to locate H-2 in the chaos of the base. . . .

Under these dramatic circumstances, I became the mother of a frail, seven-month-old, six-pound baby girl. At UCLA Medical

Center, we were told that she had suffered from malnutrition to such a degree that her liver was "palpable" and her intestinal lining had come away, distending her stomach and making it impossible for her to digest normally; she was fed through tubes going into her temples. Even after her hospitalization, she was too weak to hold up her head without support. Her scabby limbs fell like limp vines from my arms, and her cry was barely audible and without conviction. But she was luminously beautiful, and there was something in the quality of her gaze that let me know everything was going to be okay.

Henry Fonda

Henry Fonda has enjoyed huge success for his Hollywood and Broadway roles in a career that spanned more than forty-five years. Raised in Omaha, Nebraska, he studied journalism before seeking success as an actor. In 1929, Fonda debuted on Broadway, and he began appearing in dramatic movie roles six years later, often directed by the acclaimed John Ford. Among Fonda's best-known films are *The Grapes of Wrath, Fort Apache, Twelve Angry Men, Once Upon a Time in the West*, and *On Golden Pond*, for which he won an Academy Award. Fonda was already ailing with heart disease when this film was made—

he died soon after its release—and for many critics, it was his crowning achievement.

In his memoir *Fonda, My Life*, readers were offered this fatherly reminiscence:

> Susan couldn't get pregnant, and she and I both wanted a [third] child very much. Nedda and Josh Legan helped us to make arrangements.
>
> A doctor called on the phone one day and gave us the news. "The baby has been born and is in a foster home in Connecticut. If you want we'll have the foster parents bring her to the adoption home. You can change your mind, if you like. You can say no."
>
> It was a terribly emotional day. We hired a limousine and a driver to take us to the place. An attendant showed us to a small room and told us to wait. The wait seemed eternal.
>
> Suddenly, a door opened and a nurse came in carrying this eight-week-old baby in her arms. We fell in love with that right then and I said, "No way are we going to leave without her!"
>
> In the car, we took turns holding the baby. When we arrived at our new house on East Seventy Fourth Street, we whisked her up to the nursery. We were completely prepared. Susan even had a nurse's name ready to call. Everything was set. We named the baby Amy, and let me tell you. I have to be reminded that she's an adopted child. She's our own.

Something else wonderful about having Amy. I'd never had a chance to be a proper father to Jane or Peter when they were infants. I hadn't been allowed to touch them. But now, with Amy, I used to be the one who got up at five o'clock in the morning. I gave her the bottles and I burped her. I just had a ball!

Jacquelyn Mitchard

Jacqueline Mitchard is a novelist and syndicated columnist whose column, "The Rest of Us," is featured in newspapers across the country. Her first fictional work, *The Deep End of the Ocean*, was a New York Times best-seller, chosen as the first book for Oprah Winfrey's Book Club, and made into a movie starring Michelle Pfeiffer and Treat Williams. Mitchard has also served as a speechwriter for Donna Shalala, former secretary of the Department of Health and Human Services in the Clinton administration; her other books include *A Theory of Relativity* and *The Most Wanted*.

Mitchard is the mother of four adopted children; in *The Adoption Reader*, she shared this recollection:

Twenty hours later, my husband and I were in a crowded Chicago hospital, picking our way nervously down corridors to the maternity floor, expecting to be stopped at any moment. The

 51

nun gave me a measuring look when I asked for Amy. She was still in isolation, and no one but close family was allowed in the room when the baby was present. But as I learned from a hospital social worker, the nun knew exactly who we were and decided to let God work it out.

She showed us to a cramped little room. Amy was sitting on the bed in a blue peignoir set that would have been right at home in an old Doris Day movie. Her hair was brick red; I knew right away that she had called it auburn to sound more sophisticated. She looked up. She was a pretty woman, with freckles and a generous mouth and the oddest color eyes—neither brown nor hazel but just like a leaf just beginning to turn in the fall.

"Jack?" she said, using the nickname I had heard so often on the phone. My throat was too full for me to do anything but nod. She stood up and came into my arms. We held each other silently. My husband put his arms around us both.

Then she turned to the Plexiglass bassinet that had been partially hidden behind her. She reached in and picked up a baby as big and bonny and rosy dark as I had imagined him. "Look, Danny," she said, "I told you Mommy and Daddy were coming."

My husband made a sound somewhere between a cough and a sob. Amy placed Danny in my arms.

As I nuzzled the baby, she crowed over him like any proud

mother. "Isn't he beautiful?" she said. "See how big he is? See? He knows it's you. He smiled."

I was lost in him. The bonds radiated from him and locked me fast. . . . Amy had not broken her trust. I appreciated it then. I'm awestruck by it now.

Amy and I traded Danny back and forth. Then his new father held him. "Oh, thank you," Dan said over and over. "Thank you. Thank you." It sounded like a prayer.

Rosie O'Donnell

Actress, comedienne, and talk show host, Rosie O'Donnell grew up on Long Island during the 1960s and '70s. After suffering at age ten the loss of her mother from cancer, Rosie often found solace in watching movies and TV, finding idols and role models in Lucille Ball, Barbra Streisand, Carol Burnett, and Bette Midler. After graduating as high school president, prom queen, and homecoming queen, O'Donnell embarked on a grand tour of the United States. She made five winning appearances on *Star Search* before moving to Los Angeles in 1984. She spent four years as host of VH-1's most popular show, *Stand-Up Spotlight*, before launching into films, starting with *A League of their Own*, followed by *Sleepless in Seattle, Another Stakeout*, and others including *Now and Then, Harriet the Spy*, and *Wide Awake*.

In 1996, O'Donnell accepted a post as host of syndicated variety talk show *The Rosie O'Donnell Show*, featuring such attractions as celebrity guests and Broadway performances. Inspired by *The Merv Griffin Show*, O'Donnell pitted her amiable, cozy attitude against the swarm of sensationalist programs dominating the airwaves. Today, she is best known in the public eye for her three adoptions as a single woman, and for promoting the adoptive process through her non-profit organization, Rosie Adoptions.

In her memoir, *Find Me*, O'Donnell shared this adoptive experience:

I was on the kitchen floor cleaning out the fridge when the phone rang. The social worker, knowing I was ready for a girl, had that tone of voice that raises neck hairs, happy but wanting. Something was wrong. I was in a panic . . . did the birth mother change her mind? My heart was pounding. I had to fight to stay in my body. "Is there a problem? What's the problem?"

"No problem," she said, "You have a healthy son."

She must have said more, but I didn't hear it. Son? A boy. I had a boy. How could that be? I was fairly certain I was supposed to have a girl. Not because of my sonogram but because I thought God wanted me to have a girl. I had dead-mother stuff to work out, surely my life lessons would be learned through my daughter. A boy, what would I do with a boy? There must have been a pause, because the social worker asked, "Are you okay? Any questions?"

"Yeah," I said. "When he is coming home?"

He spent the night in the hospital; I spent mine wide-awake, unable to sleep for even a moment. . . . I paced the floors and watched for the blue Volvo station wagon that held my son—the moment I knew would completely alter my life.

I thought I was prepared; no one ever is. The doorbell rang. I opened the door and saw a tiny yellow blanket with slick matted black hair sticking straight up. I reached for him, as he did me. When he was in my arms, he opened his eyes. Black-blue pools of steel staring right into me. Hi Mama, I heard inside, Here we go. . . .

My baby is now a first-grader. I am a fun but strict mom. . . . Nothing happens by chance. I have a son—in fact, now I have two. I have learned not to second-guess God. Things are not always as they seem. There are treasures right beneath our eyes.

This boy of mine has brought me to a new level of loving, beyond the beyond. A place I had dreamed of, but never knew was real.

Hi Mama, here we go.

Barbara Walters

Barbara Walters is among America's most admired TV reporters and anchors for her ability to humanize the news, including complex geopolitical events. The Boston-raised Walters began her career on NBC's *Today* show, moving up the ladder from writer and researcher to an on-screen Today Girl to the morning show's first female host. In 1976, Walters signed with ABC to become the first woman to anchor the nightly network news, but left three years later to become a correspondent for *20/20* and eventually its co-anchor. Her other TV work includes *The Barbara Walters Show*, for which she won one of her numerous Emmys, and *The View*. A feature for *Ladies Home Journal* highlighted her adoptive experience:

Walters, a woman not given to public displays of emotion, described the first time she held her adopted daughter in her arms:

"That's the thing about adoption that most surprised me: how the second this child is in your arms, she is yours. Not only for me, but for my family—my mother and father and sister. The power of that love! . . .

"My daughter and I would be splashing in the tub—I loved taking baths with her—and I said, 'There are two ways mom-

mies have babies. Sometimes they carry them in their tummy'—
I know 'tummy' is politically incorrect today, but that's what I
said—'and sometimes a mommy can't carry a baby in her
tummy. So she carries hers in her heart. You were adopted, so
you were born in my heart.'

"Make sure you really want a baby, and you aren't just doing
it because society says you should, because it changes your life.

"You've got to be comfortable with the idea that the child may
not have your mannerisms or even your way of thinking about
the world. But on the other hand, she won't have your bad
habits, either.

"Your adopted child may not be perfect, but then neither
would your biological child. Even though I'm a terribly religious
person, I feel that this child was born for me."

Being a Celebrity Dad

Will Smith

Will Smith is among the few American entertainers to achieve resounding success in both pop music and film. Growing up in middle-class West Philadelphia, he started rapping when he was a pre-teen and turned down an MIT scholarship to pursue a performing career. Smith was a millionaire by the time he was eighteen, and two years later, he and Jeff Townes had produced two platinum albums. Starting his acting career with six years on the popular TV sitcom *Fresh Prince of Bel-Air*, Smith gained his first major film role in *Six Degrees of Separation*, followed by *Independence Day, Men in Black, Men in Black 2*, and the critically acclaimed *Ali*, for which he gained an Oscar nomination for his starring performance portraying boxer Muhammad Ali.

Smith is married to actress Jada Pinkett and they have two sons. In a recent interview for *Back Stage West*, Smith remarked:

I definitely want to be more than an actor. I want to be more important than that. I want the world to be different because I was here. . . . I think a large part of [my ability to connect as an actor] is my upbringing. I was raised as a Baptist. I went to Catholic school. I lived in a Jewish neighborhood and played with the Muslim kids that lived in the next neighborhood. I went to Catholic school for nine years with all white people, and then for high school, I went to Overbrook High, which was all black people. So I think I have a really accurate picture, a cross-section of America.

I was in Sydney, Australia, with my three-year-old son, Jaden, who really hasn't experienced any of my work. We are in this shopping mall, and a woman comes up to me and asks for my autograph. I sign it, and she walks away. My son stops and looks at me, and says, "Who are you, Daddy?"

Being a Celebrity Mom

Gillian Anderson

Gillian Anderson is best known for playing investigator Dana Scully in the science fiction TV series *The X-Files*. Born in Chicago and brought up in London, she returned with her family to the United States, studying at DePaul University and gaining theater roles in New York City before getting her big TV break. At the time, nobody connected with *The X-Files* could have imagined it would last for nine seasons and gain international cult status. For all her television success, Anderson has not abandoned the stage, and she recently appeared in the film version of Edith Wharton's *The House of Mirth*.

Los Angeles Magazine highlighted Anderson in a feature interview:

Most of the little free time that Anderson has is spent trying to give Piper as normal a childhood as possible. Over the summer hiatus, she and her daughter traveled to London and reveled in riding the subway without being recognized. "I will not take her to premieres," Anderson comments. "When she's around, I run in the other direction if I see somebody approaching for an autograph. I just don't want her to witness me being special in any way."

Meryl Streep

Nominated for twelve Oscars in twenty-two years, Meryl Streep has now tied Katherine Hepburn for the greatest total number of acting Academy Award nominations. After graduating from the Yale School of Drama in 1975, she moved to New York City and soon began working with Joseph Papp's Public Theater. In 1977, Streep made her film debut in *Julia*, playing alongside Jane Fonda and Vanessa Redgrave. Over the next few years, she quickly gained blockbuster status with such movies as *The Deer Hunter, Kramer vs. Kramer*, and *Sophie's Choice*; subsequent hits included *Silkwood* and *Out of Africa*. After her performing popularity dropped during the early 1990s, Streep underwent a career renaissance with such films as *The Bridges of Madison County, Dancing at Lughnasa,* and the emotionally harrowing *One True Thing,* in which she played a woman dying of cancer. Although *Music of the Heart* was largely panned by critics, it generated yet another Oscar nomination for Streep, who also starred in the critically acclaimed *Adaptation* and *The Hours*. Streep lives lakeside in rural Connecticut with her sculptor husband, Don Gummer, and their four children.

In an interview for *Good Housekeeping*, Streep observed:

It's a choice of protecting your kids. Young actresses who have babies don't know this. I've learned over time that if you have your picture taken with your baby, you have put your baby under the umbrella of your fame. That removes their protection, their civil rights under the law. I don't have any rights as a celebrity. They can write whatever they want about me—and they do. But if somebody slanders, misrepresents, or writes something untrue about my child, I have recourse to defend them. If I have publicized them in my pictures, they don't have any protection.

Children have a right to their lives. I have a deep understanding of how my fame has affected my brothers and their children, who have my last name. It's this [effluvia] trailing from the back of the car, like a tin can. "Oh, are you related to her?" It's a drag for them. Because they don't want to be different.

People [who approach me] are always very nice. But my children really hate it. I try to explain to them, "This is the first time this person has met somebody famous. It may be the gazillionth time you've been approached when you're with me. But the encounter is different for a stranger than it is for us. Try to be more compassionate. And just get over yourself. . . . This is your handicap."

Building Your Child's Character

Abigail Adams

Abigail Adams has a unique place in American history, one shared with Barbara Bush. An influential patriot during the Revolutionary War, she was married to one president (John Adams) and mother to a second (John Quincy Adams). Born in Weymouth, Massachusetts, to a family of Congregational ministers, Abigail lacked formal education, as did other women of her time. But her curiosity sparked her keen intelligence, and she read widely.

Long separations kept Abigail from her beloved husband, John, while he served as delegate to the Continental Congress, envoy abroad, and elected officer under the newly crafted Constitution. The two were married for more than fifty years and raised five children.

In September 1774, Abigail penned John these pensive words:

> I have always thought it of great importance that children should, in the early part of life, be unaccustomed to such exam-

ples as would tend to corrupt the purity of their words and actions that they may chill with horror at the sound of an oath and blush with indignation at an obscene expression. These first principals, which grow with their growth and strengthen with their strength neither time or custom can totally eradicate.

Katie Couric

Katie Couric is among the world's most highly paid TV personalities. Graduating from the University of Virginia with a degree in American Studies in 1979, she began her career as a desk assistant at ABC, where she worked under anchorman Sam Donaldson, among others. Shortly thereafter, Couric started at the Washington bureau of the fledgling Cable News Network (CNN) and then did stints as a producer and open-air reporter at various CNN bureaus around the country.

As co-anchor of NBC's morning newsmagazine *Today*, Couric became an instant hit in the early '90s, combining a pleasant, charming demeanor with a surprisingly hard-hitting journalistic style. She gained coveted interviews with leaders in the public eye, including First Lady Hillary Rodham Clinton, George Bush, Colin Powell, and Jerry Seinfeld. In 1998, following the death of her forty-two-year-old husband, Jay Monahan, from colon cancer, Couric aggressively raised millions for research. Two years later, her children's book, *The Brand New Kid*, topped the New York Times children's picture-book best-seller list for weeks.

Good Housekeeping recently featured an interview with Couric:

Like parents around the country, she worries about the effect the consumer culture is having on her kids. For years, Katie has been known as extremely frugal (a recent gossip column made much of the fact that during a family trip she and the girls flew Jet-Blue, a low-cost airline, and Katie packed sandwiches for the trip herself).

But the penny-pincher label is one that bothers her. "It's about value, and also about being taken advantage of, and spending your money on the wrong things," she says emphatically. But living, as she does, in a city bursting with much of the nation's wealth, she struggles to keep her kids from wanting, wanting, wanting.

"Ellie asked for a Baby G watch a couple of years ago, when those were very big with kids. It was $95, and I thought that was extravagant for a second grader. But there were kids in her class who had three of them!" (For the record, Ellie never got one).

Choosing Parenthood

Benjamin Spock

Benjamin Spock was America's most beloved pediatrician through much of the twentieth century. His *Baby and Child Care*, in its first year of publication in 1941, was an immediate success through sheer word-of-mouth, and became a "bible" for millions of parents. Eventually translated into dozens of languages, *Baby and Child Care* began with these encouraging words: "Trust yourself. You know more than you think you do."

The eldest of six children, Spock was born in New England in the early 1900s, in an era of gas lamps and horse carriages. As a youngster, he was exceedingly shy and timid; only after winning a gold medal in the 1924 Olympics, rowing with the Yale crew, did he begin to become confident in his own abilities. After medical school, Spock became the first physician ever to train in both pediatrics and psychoanalysis.

Later, when seeking to build up his struggling practice in Depression-era New York City, Spock was invited to write a parenting manual. His editor's advice: "It doesn't have to be very good, we're only going to charge a quarter."

As cited by Bill Adler in his anthology *Motherhood, A Celebration*, the famed pediatrician wisely noted:

Of course, parents don't have children because they want to be martyrs, or at least they shouldn't. They have them because they love children and want some of their very own. They also love children because they remember being loved so much by their parents in their childhood. Taking care of their children, seeing them grow and develop into fine people, gives most parents—despite the hard work—their greatest satisfaction in life.

Congratulating a New Father

John Adams

As the second U.S. president, John Adams was more remarkable as a political philosopher than as a politician. A Harvard-educated lawyer, he became a leader of the American revolution and served two frustrating terms as vice president—which he famously called "the most insignificant office that ever the invention of man contrived or his imagination conceived"—before gaining the new nation's highest post in 1797.

Adams was already the father of babies Abigail Amelia and future president John Quincy when, in September 1767, he jovially wrote to a friend:

> I have but a few moments to congratulate you on the fresh blessing to your family—another fine child and sister comfortable! Oh fine! I know the feeling as well as you, and in spite of your

earlier marriage, I knew it sooner than you. Here you must own I have the advantage of you. But what shall we do with this young fry?

In a little while, Johnny must go to college and Nabby must have fine clothes, aye, and so must Betsy too and the other and all the rest. And very cleverly you and I shall feel when we recollect that we are hard at work, over watches and lawsuits, and Johnny and Betsy at the same time raking and fluttering away our profits. Aye, and there must be dancing schools and boarding schools and all that, or else, you know, we shall not give them polite educations—and they will better not have been born than not have polite educations!

Coping with a Prolonged Pregnancy

Hunter Tylo

Hunter Tylo (born Deborah Jo Hunter) is one of America's most popular daytime TV actresses. Besides hosting a syndicated parenting talk show, *First Priority*, she has starred on programs including *The Bold and the Beautiful, All My Children*, and *Days of Our Lives*. Among her movie credits are *The Jack of All Trades*. Tylo began her professional life as a ten-year-old child model in Dallas. After her teenage marriage ended, Hunter moved to New York City to pursue her acting career and met her husband-to-be, actor Michael Tylo, in the soap opera *All My Children*. Recently, Hunter created a charity called Hunter's Chosen Child to aid pregnant women and families with services such as day care scholarships.

In her best-selling autobiography, *Making a Miracle*, the popular actress recalled her son Michael Tylo II's birth:

As I continued with my studies [at Fordham University] the next spring, I began to experience a lot of weariness in the last stages of pregnancy. I told the doctor that this was going to be a *huge* baby. She assured me that every woman felt that way.

My parents arrived at our apartment near the due date in early April and the baby watch began. They were still there two weeks after my due date. "We're going home if this baby doesn't come soon," my mother teased me. I started feeling more and more overwhelmed by carrying around all that weight. On April 21, I took to my bed and stayed there for two days, depressed, unable and unwilling to get up.

My parents and Michael concocted a scheme to send me into labor. My mother insisted I get up. She helped me get dressed and did my hair. Michael then took me on a walk down to Lincoln Center, a good twenty blocks away. My mother thought a walk might kick labor into gear, but nothing happened.

When we got back, Michael and my parents ordered in barbecue ribs and potato salad, the greasy, gooey food I like best. I had felt so full from the baby pressing on my stomach that I had pretty much stopped eating. But I went to the table and tasted a rib or two.

Then I went over and sat down on the couch. Chris came

bouncing out from his room after a long nap. "Mom's up!" he cried. He ran to me and jumped into my lap with his knees pulled up, crashing his head into my chest.

"Ow!" I couldn't think for a moment for the pain.

He scrambled off but stayed right before me. "Mom," he said, his eyes huge. "You're *wet*. Your water broke. Mom's water broke! *Mom's water broke!*" Now he was screaming it. . . .

My water had broken about 7:30 P.M. My contractions stopped about 10:00 P.M. This had happened with Chris, too. My labor progressed up to a point, then tapered off and quit. [After I got to the hospital] the doctors and nurses insisted that I walk to get the labor started again, and my . . . husband and I hobbled up and down the corridors supporting one another. As I was passing one of the rooms, I noticed that *Saturday Night Live* was ending. It was almost 1:00 A.M.

Coping with Medical Circumcision

Kathie Lee Gifford

Television personality and singer Kathie Lee Gifford is best known as longtime co-host of TV's *Live with Regis & Kathie Lee*, as well as a pop performer whose recent albums include *Heart of a Woman, Born for You*, and a collection of children's songs called *Party Animals*. As a former gospel singer, Kathie Lee successfully weathered a marital scandal involving her husband, football announcer Frank Gifford, which initially damaged her image as a doting wife and mother of two. Besides serving as a spokesperson for a variety of consumer-product companies, she has produced her own fitness video and runs two charity organizations.

In her autobiography *I Can't Believe I Said That!* Kathie Lee Gifford reminisced:

> The morning of the birth, Uncle Regis finally had his big scoop. He made the announcement on the air, with Joy filling in for

 73

me. Then he got me on the phone in my hospital room. I was real groggy and my speech was slurred. "I'm holding the most precious little boy," I said. I was about as cognizant as a human can be on morphine. "You find out every woman, every pregnancy, every little baby's so unique." I said. "It was an experience I will never forget. A gift from God, that's the only thing you can say. . . ."

I wasn't long before I had to face a more traumatic "C" than my own "C" (section): Cody's circumcision.

I couldn't bear the thought of my child leaving my arms, much less going under the knife. To deal with my anxiety, I nursed Cody right before, wrote this little note, and stuck it in his diaper:

> Dear Dr. Langan:
>
> Just take a tad.
> Please leave me most of what I already had.
> Life is too short, so don't make ME that way!
> Now please hold steady and have a nice day.
>
> Love, Cody

In the forty years of Dr. Langan's practice, no one had ever left a message in a baby's diaper. The nurse said it was so funny that the doctor screamed. I wanted the note back for Cody's baby book, but [the doctor] said, "Make your own copy." The nurse told me Cody didn't even cry and that it was the best circumcision Dr. Langan had ever done—of course. Painless and perfect.

Coping with Stubborn Tots

Faith Hill

Singer and songwriter Faith Hill is known for such country hit singles as "This Kiss," "Breathe," and "Just to Hear You Say You Love Me." An adopted child raised in Jackson, Mississippi, she gained her first singing experience as a child in her family's Baptist church. As a young teenager, Hill learned to play guitar, and by age sixteen she had started her own country band, playing at local fairs and rodeos. Moving to Nashville to achieve greater success, she was spotted by a Warner/Reprise scout while performing at a popular club. In 1993, Hill's debut album, *Take Me as I Am*, gained her immediate honors, including Best Female Country Artist from *Billboard* and *Performance* magazines. Subsequent albums have included *It Matters to Me, Faith*, the triple-platinum *Breathe*, and, most recently, *Cry*. Married to country performer Tim McGraw, Faith Hill has set up a Family Literacy Project charity that bears her name.

In an interview for *Good Housekeeping*, Faith Hill remarked:

[With three young children], our house is always a little wild. But you just have to let your feet hit the ground running and think, *Well, okay, this has to be a joyful day, because this is absolutely out of control.*

We're always trying to figure out lots of things, especially how to get them to eat. We called up our pediatrician and asked, "What if they don't want to eat? Nothing at all?" And he said: "Then don't give them anything."

Oh, yeah. I've gone the milk shake route sometimes.

Even for breakfast. I've said, "Okay, so you're not going to eat anything. How about a milk shake?" Just to put something in their little bellies. But, you know, everyone assures me that when they're hungry, they'll eat. And I guess that's right.

Cutting the Umbilical Cord

Kevin Sorbo

Kevin Sorbo spent three years traveling around the world, modeling for print ads and appearing in more than 150 commercials before landing in his breakout TV series *Hercules*. Raised in small-town Minnesota where he excelled at high school football, baseball, and basketball, Sorbo joined an actors' theater group after graduating from college. His performances spanned Europe and Australia. After settling in Los Angeles, the tall and muscular Sorbo began appearing on such popular TV shows as *Murder She Wrote*.

After starring in the title role of *Hercules: The Legendary Journeys*, Sorbo became internationally famous and learned the filmmaking craft well enough to direct and co-write some of the episodes. He followed *Hercules* with a starring role in the science fiction series *Andromeda*. He currently devotes much of his time to A World for

Fit Kids!, a program that trains inner-city teens to become mentors via sports for younger children.

In "By Zeus, It's a Boy," *TV Star* magazine highlighted:

On the evening of August 21st, the six-foot-three former model was exercising at his home outside Las Vegas when his wife, actress Sam Jenkins Sorbo, poked her head in. "Honey, how much longer do you have on the treadmill?" she asked.

"About eighteen minutes," he replied. Then as Sorbo recalls, "I said, 'What's wrong?' She said, 'Well, my water just broke.'"

The next afternoon, Sorbo stood beside Sam in a hospital delivery room and, supervised by her obstetrician, prepared to sever the umbilical cord of their first child, Braeden Cooper. "I was crying at first," says the actor, "I said to the doctor, 'Make sure I cut the right thing, because I can't see.'"

Deciding to Be a Mother

Sigourney Weaver

Best known for starring in the *Alien* film trilogy, Sigourney (née Susan) is the daughter of British actress Elizabeth Inglis and NBC president Sylvester Weaver. She studied at the Yale School of Drama, where she performed in stage productions with Meryl Streep and befriended playwright Christopher Durang. After occasional Broadway and TV appearances, and a six-second appearance as Woody Allen's movie date in *Annie Hall*, Weaver gained immediate fame as the embattled heroine of *Alien*. Aside from the three popular sequels, her subsequent films have included *Working Girl, Gorillas in the Mist, Dave, The Ice Storm*, and *Map of the World*—the latter two gained her Golden Globe nominations for Best Actress and Best Supporting Actress, respectively. Married to stage director James Simpson, Weaver postponed motherhood until she was forty.

In an interview for *People* weekly, she intriguingly commented:

"Whether it was work, marriage, or family, I've always been a late bloomer. It was a matter of being ready, and I made a deliberate decision to cut back on work. I've made only six films in the last five years. After all, if you bungle bringing up your children, it doesn't really matter what you do with the rest of your life."

Debra Winger

The daughter of a kosher frozen-food distributor, Debra Winger quit high school at the age of sixteen to join an Israeli kibbutz. After returning to the United States, she studied social science in California before choosing an acting career. Winger's first taste of fame came as the super-powered younger sister of Lynda Carter in the fantasy TV series *Wonder Woman*. In the 1980s, she catapulted to stardom with such films as *Urban Cowboy, An Officer and a Gentleman, Legal Eagles*, and *Terms of Endearment* with Shirley MacLaine, which won her an Oscar nomination. Though garnering critical praise for her roles in such later movies as *The Sheltering Sky, Shadowlands*, and *Forget Paris*, Winger has clearly devoted more attention to raising her three children in suburban New York City than to expanding her acting career.

For a *People* magazine cover story on actresses as mothers, Winger confided:

 81

"I think there's a natural cycle in a woman's life that is somewhat in tune with her body. You look at your life and say, "Do I want to do the same thing for the second half that I did for the first? I feel different. Maybe I should *be* different."

Displaying Fatherly Affection

Kirk Douglas

Kirk Douglas is considered by many to be the epitome of the Hollywood hard man. Besides appearing in dozens of films over more than half a century, Douglas has served as director and producer, and he will forever be associated with his role in ending the infamous Hollywood black list. Born as Issur Danielovitch to Russian-Jewish immigrant parents in New York City, he worked briefly as a professional wrestler after completing college and before pursuing an acting career. Following active service in the U.S. Navy during World War II, Douglas debuted on film in 1946, but first gained popularity three years later with his portrayal of an unscrupulous boxer in *Champion*.

Thanks to strong roles in such '50s classics as *Ace in the Hole, Detective Story*, and *Gunfight at the O.K. Corral*, he established his screen persona and earned Oscar nominations for his performances in *The Bad and the Beautiful* and *Lust for Life*. In 1981, Douglas won the

Presidential Medal of Freedom, the highest civilian award given in the United States, and he later authored two novels and an autobiography. Although a debilitating stroke in 1995 curtailed his activities, Douglas has recovered sufficiently to continue his acting career in *Diamonds*.

For an article in *Interview* magazine, Douglas commented:

When I kiss my sons on the mouth, people are sometimes afraid of this affection, this closeness. They look at closeness as a weakness when it should be very gratifying. When a boy is young, he likes physical contact with his father as well as his mother. I think that need is always there and you must express it. As you get more and more secure as a person, it's easier to follow those sorts of instincts.

Enjoying Fatherhood

Theodore Roosevelt

Theodore Roosevelt was the youngest man ever to become U.S. president. (He was forty-two when McKinley was assassinated in 1901.) Roosevelt grew up frail and sickly with asthma, and as a child suffered his father's early death. With his mother's encouragement, he deliberately strengthened himself by vigorous exercise and sports. Later, as an admired Rough Rider and an influential political leader for a generation, he made the phrase "speak softly and carry a big stick" famous and counseled his children to "hit the line hard." Yet Roosevelt always valued character and intelligence more than physical prowess.

Writing from the White House to his mother-in-law in January 1904, he offered these warm impressions:

> Kermie is a darling little fellow, so soft and sweet. As for blessed Ted, he is just as much of a comfort as he ever was. I think he

 85

really loves me, and when I come back after an absence, he greets me with wild enthusiasm, due however, I fear, in great part to knowledge that I am sure to have a large paper bundle of toys—which produce the query of "Fats in de bag," while he dances like an expectant little bear.

When I come in to afternoon tea, he and Alice sidle hastily round to my chair, knowing that I will surreptitiously give them all the icing off the cake if I can get Edith's attention attracted elsewhere; and every evening I have a wild romp with them, usually assuming the role of a "very big bear," while they are either little bears, or a "raccoon and a badger, papa."

Ted has a most warm, tender, loving heart; but I think he is a manly little fellow too. In fact, I take the utmost possible enjoyment out of my three children, and so does Edith.

Jerry Seinfeld

Jerry Seinfeld's brand of "observational humor" has made him one of America's most popular and imitated comedians. Born in Brooklyn, raised in suburban Massapequa ("It's an old Indian name that means 'by the mall'"), Seinfeld began the comedy club circuit the night after he graduated from Queens College. He performed stand-up for free at times just to perfect his act. Seinfeld's big break came when he became a regular guest on *Late Night with David Letterman* and the *Tonight* show. Network and cable specials followed, and in 1990 he was given the creative outlet of a lifetime: his own network sitcom. After nine successful seasons, Seinfeld decided to end the program—which won a 1993 Emmy for best comedy series—and pursue other creative activities, including marriage and child-rearing. In a *People* weekly article, Seinfeld humorously celebrated fatherhood:

> "When your eyes meet those eyes, I never loved anyone so much at first meeting. But! Let's make no mistake why these babies come here: To replace us. We'll see who's wearing the diapers when all this is over."

The magazine added:

Seinfeld lulls Sascha to sleep with an old Cracker Jack jingle. "That one little girl laughing," he told *The New York Times*, "is better than 3,000 people."

John Travolta

Actor and producer John Travolta grew up in suburban New Jersey in a family that encouraged creative expression; his older sister, Ellen, was a TV actress. His first public performance came at the age of eight, when he danced the "Twist" for a local theater crowd; immediately after high school, Travolta pursued an acting career full-time. After appearing in many commercials and stage shows, including an early road version of *Grease*, Travolta achieved his first major role in 1975 on the TV sitcom *Welcome Back, Kotter*. Two years later, his career ignited when *Saturday Night Fever* was released to both critical and popular acclaim.

After the film version of *Grease* quickly brought additional renown, Travolta slumped and struggled for years to regain his popularity—finally doing so when *Pulp Fiction* soared to success in 1994. Since then, his many well-received movies have included *Face/Off, Michael, Phenomenon, Get Shorty*, and *A Civil Action*. He and actress Kelly Preston have two children: a son, Jett, followed eight years later by a daughter, Ella Bleu.

In an interview for *Good Housekeeping*, Travolta happily mused:

I always looked forward to having a girl because there is a different sort of chemistry. I don't know how to explain it, but there's a way a girl will adore her father that is kind and unconditional. And I'm looking forward to being adored unconditionally. . . .

I was the baby in my family—my mother had me at forty-three—and I certainly know what it's like to be doted on. And I think that the day Ella was born was the best gift in the world for [eight-year-old Jett], because suddenly, he became a little bit more like your average child. . . .

I said to Jett recently, "You know, I think this baby is a good thing. Because now we're going to get to do more of what we want to do without all the girls telling us how to do it, when to do it, and where to do it. We can stay up a little longer. We can go for longer rides. We can take a break from gym classes sometimes, or school, and do things, just the two of us, without someone constantly looking over our shoulders."

[With my kids], I'm completely a pushover. Other than protecting them from hurting themselves, there are no rules. But I can't help it because I don't feel like I was brought up with that many rules. You know, my parents had five kids already by the time I was born, and they were so tolerant of me, and I was very demanding and very outspoken.

Robin Williams

Robin Williams is among Hollywood's most popular film actors. The son of a Ford Motor Company executive, Williams moved frequently with his parents, and as a pudgy only child he used a prodigious imagination to keep himself happily amused. Originally training in New

York City to be a serious actor, he began performing stand-up comedy routines in California clubs during the mid-70s. Williams starred in the TV hit *Mork and Mindy*, in which he played a crazy space alien.

After a string of unsuccessful movies, Williams gained wide popularity and an Oscar nomination with *Good Morning, Vietnam* in 1984. He garnered two more Oscar nominations for *Dead Poets Society* and *The Fisher King*, respectively. Though not all of Williams's films have generated either critical acclaim or box-office largesse, his successes have been many—including the manic genie voice for *Aladdin,* and his roles in *Mrs. Doubtfire, Patch Adams, What Dreams May Come*, and *Good Will Hunting*, which gained him an Oscar for Best Supporting Actor. In addition to his considerable filmwork, Williams has recorded three albums, appeared in a multitude of TV comedy specials, and since the '80s has been a primary host of *Comic Relief*, an annually televised benefit for the homeless. He has three children. In an interview for *Ladies Home Journal*, Williams observed:

[The key to being a good parent involves] a weird combination. You have to be there when they need you, and then you have to be able to back away. It's knowing when to step forward and intervene and when not to say, "Oh, the baby's got a knife, how cute!"

In an earlier interview for *Time*, Williams commented:

I watch Zachary absorbed in playing with his rockets, I listen to him whispering his multiple voices, and I think, "That's where it comes from. That's the source."

To [*Time* writer Richard] Corliss, Williams related a story of Zachary at his "gestalt" day care center.

The teacher was playing tapes of noises for the kids to identify. One was of a baby crying, and a little girl said, "That's a baby crying." Then they played a tape of laughter. "I know, I know!" Zachary said, "That's comedy!" And I thought: "Right on!"

Enjoying Motherhood

Cindy Crawford

During the 1980s and '90s Cindy Crawford was America's most cele-brated fashion model, embodying the rise of the "supermodel" as a new cultural phenomenon. No longer nameless faces on magazine covers, calendars, and fashion runways, they had become celebrities whose fame rivaled that of movie stars and rock musicians. Cindy Crawford stood at the forefront of this insurgence, winning in 1982—at age sixteen—the "Look of the Year" contest sponsored by the Elite Modeling Agency. Within months, the statuesque (five-foot, nine-and-a-half-inch, 130-pound) model was featured on the cover of *Vogue*. After years of successful involvement in fitness videos, TV specials, commercial endorsements, and film, Crawford has relatively settled down in the Los Angeles area with husband restauranteur-entrepreneur Rande Gerber to raise their two children, Presley and Kaia.

In a cover story for *Ladies Home Journal*, Crawford related:

It's really great watching the man you love become a father. . . ."
My sister told me the one thing about having kids is you don't have to figure out your priorities anymore, because you're looking at them. It's so true. . . .
"Now that Presley is starting to talk, we actually have conversations. I knew I would love my child, but I didn't know that I would have fun hanging out with a two-year-old. Being one of three girls, I can't imagine not having one.

Namjo Kim

Namjo Kim ranks among South Korea's most respected poets today. Born in Daegu, she authored her first book of verse, *Life*, in 1953, with subsequent volumes that have included *Tree and Wind, Flag of Passions, For You*, and *Ending Pain and Endless Love*. Winning several national prizes for her poetry, Namjo Kim currently teaches at Sukmyong Women's University. For more than fifty years, her writing has highlighted such themes as maternal affection and life's simple joys. The following poem is drawn from her 1958 collection, *Tree and Wind*, and appears in the anthology *Selected Poems of Namjo Kim,* edited and translated by David McCann and Hyunjae Ye Sallee.

CHILD AND MOTHER NAPPING

Daytime, eyes drooping,
for a moment mother
holding her child's hand as both sleep:

The child's face,
Smooth as the round moon in the water;
eyes half-closed, half
open, gleaming faintly.

Like flowers bunched in clusters
or a basket full of well-ripened fruit,
the constant scent of flesh,
baby's smell.

Crossing the edge of dreams,
baby's mind and mother's;
call it an echo riding a golden cart,
or the spring winds
gently kissing:

As baby awakens
mother too opens her eyes;
when baby laughs, all at once
mother's heart is a sunrise.

> Outside the papered door
> Whoever might come and go,
> this place by baby's side
> is mother's paradise.

Kelly Ripa

After mastering daytime TV as a star on the soap opera *All My Children*, Kelly Ripa quickly stepped into her new role as co-host of Regis Philbin's popular morning show. The oldest daughter of a New Jersey bus driver and homemaker, Kelly began taking ballet and piano lessons at an early age. After graduating from high school, Ripa enrolled in community college, but fate had other plans in store for the budding actress: During her first week of classes, she auditioned for *All My Children*, and won a role competing against far more experienced performers. After several years on the show, in 1996 Ripa married her co-star Mark Consuelos.

Following a few appearances as guest host on Regis Philbin's morning show, in early 2001 Ripa was offered the co-host seat that had been vacated by Kathie Lee Gifford. In her first months on the *Live with Regis and Kelly* show, she shared private information about her pregnancy and life with the program's large TV audience, gaining national stardom as a result.

In an interview for *Good Housekeeping*, Kelly Ripa warmly commented:

Both of my kids came out looking just like my husband, with this jet-black hair. Lola, though, has blue eyes. And Mark, looking right at my face, actually said in amazement, "I think she has blue eyes! Where did they come from?"

I said to him, "I don't want to alarm you, but we think I'm her mother. I may have something to do with it."

My husband is so in love with Lola. Right after she was born, he went out into the hallway and shouted, "I have a daughter!" . . . and there was nobody out there. It was six in the morning! All the nurses were saying to me, "There's a new woman in his life, look out!" And it's true. He will never let her go out on a date. Never. She'll be in a convent. Michael is also very protective. "That's my sister. Don't touch her." This girl is never going to have any boyfriends.

We're much more relaxed with Lola than with our firstborn. With Michael we would make people boil themselves before they could hold him. With Lola, I'm asking taxicab drivers to hold her while I hunt for my wallet. . . .

As for losing the baby weight, I've said it before, and I'll say it again. If you want to take off your baby weight, then you should breast-feed, because it really speeds things along. Honestly, it revs up your metabolism or something. But it's odd because I always think I look so great after I give birth. Then a week later, I see the picture and I say: "Who took this of me with eight chins?"

Enjoying Pregnancy

Rosalynn Carter

"She's the girl I want to marry," announced Jimmy Carter to his mother after his first date with seventeen-year-old Rosalynn Smith, who had grown up as a friend and neighbor of the Carters in Plains, Georgia. As the oldest child of four, Rosalynn worked hard to help her mother, who became a dressmaker to support the family after the death of the children's father. At the time, Jimmy was home from the U.S. Naval Academy at Annapolis. Their romance progressed, and in 1946, they were married.

During over a half century of life together, Rosalynn helped raise their four children, advised her husband on business and political affairs, and later, as First Lady, served as the thirty-ninth president's personal emissary to Latin American countries. Currently, Rosalynn Carter is vice chair of The Carter Center in Atlanta, founded in 1982 to promote peace and human rights worldwide. Her interests include fostering programs to promote greater mental health access and promoting democracy around the globe.

In her autobiography, *The First Lady from Plains*, Rosalynn Carter reminisced:

> Soon after we returned to Norfolk, I discovered I was pregnant. Although we were elated about the baby, I was miserable, sick not only in the morning, but afternoon and night as well. Jimmy put a big box of crackers, some sliced lemon, and a pot of tea on the table by the bed before he left on Monday mornings, and somehow I survived until he came home on the weekends. This lasted the first few months, but once they were past I had no more problems.
>
> John William Carter, named after my grandfather Murray, was born on July 3, 1947. I spent our first anniversary in the hospital with our new baby son.

Cristina Garcia

Havana-born Cristina Garcia is a novelist who explores Latino family life from her bicultural vantage point. She immigrated with her family to the United States as a child and studied for a career with the Foreign Service before working as a *Time* journalist during the

1980s. Garcia's first novel, *Dreaming in Cuban*, was a 1992 finalist for the National Book Award. Her subsequent books include *The Aguero Sisters, Cars of Cuba*, and *Icubanisimo: The Vintage Book of Contemporary Cuban Literature*. In the anthology *A Question of Balance*, Garcia reflected on her pregnancy:

> I was extremely preoccupied with what was going on during [it]; instead of reading novels and poetry, I was consuming baby books. Somehow, being pregnant, I felt so centered in a different way that it didn't faze me so much. In retrospect, I look back amazed at all that has happened. While I was going through it, it was a mildly pleasant feeling, as opposed to totally excited and out-of-my-mind joy.

Barbra Streisand

As a movie actress, director, producer, singer, and stage performer, Barbra Streisand is unequalled today. Her film *The Prince of Tides* was the first motion picture directed by a woman ever to receive a Best Director nomination from the Directors Guild of America, as well as seven Academy Award nominations. Recipient of an honorary degree from Brandeis University in 1995, Barbra is a rare honoree: the only artist to earn Cable Ace, Emmy, Golden Globe, Grammy,

Oscar, Peabody, and Tony awards. With more than forty gold, twenty-five platinum, and thirteen multi-platinum albums, she continues to be the biggest-selling female recording artist ever. Her film and stage roles include *Funny Girl, What's Up Doc?, The Way We Were, For Pete's Sake*, and *A Star Is Born*.

Streisand, Her Life by biographer Anne Edwards related the following:

> "When I was pregnant, at least the last four months, I was a woman. No deadlines or curtains to meet. Whenever I thought of what was growing inside me [I felt], it's a miracle, the height of creativity for any woman."

> She had worried about morning sickness, but never experienced it. She sat around eating a lot of brownies, and her inactivity caused her to gain weight.

> "I've always had a secret desire to be fat. Skinny kids are always being pestered about eating—especially if you have a Jewish mother." She was delighted, but her pediatrician wasn't. The weight gain was excessive, he thought, and he told Barbra to watch her calories. "My first diet!" she marveled.

Gloria Vanderbilt

Gloria Vanderbilt has been a major figure in New York City's socialite world for more than half a century. As both a fashion designer—she promoted her jeans with the aphorism "My bottoms are tops"—and a mother, she has been awarded the Gold Medal of Merit from the National Society of Arts and Letters and the Talbot Perkins Children's Services Mother of the Year Award. Helping to capitalize on the fame of her brand, she even appeared in a designer-studded episode of TV's *Love Boat* with her friend, pianist Bobby Short.

In 1988, Vanderbilt suffered great tragedy when her twenty-three-year-old son Carter died from an adverse reaction to asthma medication. In her well-received memoir, *A Mother's Story*, Vanderbilt recounted that event, and others far happier:

> The house in which our children was born was on East Sixty-Seventh Street in New York—a five-story graystone reminiscent of a house in Paris where I had lived as a child. Two stone lion sculptures we found in a New Jersey quarry were placed on either side of the stone columns of the entrance. Inside, we wanted to make the house look as if it had been there always and would be there forever, a house that had been in a family for generations—our family.

To be pregnant has been for me each time the supreme joy. It is my greatest achievement, and it is hard for me to understand women who sometimes complain about the discomfort and loss of self-image they experience when they are pregnant, because I never felt so centered, so beautiful, so loved, so important. I loved my body and my spirit as never before. Each day came as a miracle. There was not a moment when I didn't feel my best self. I was doing the greatest thing in the world without having to do anything—all I had to do was *be*.

Experiencing Labor

Roseanne

The TV actress and director Roseanne is best known for the long-running comedy that bore her name. Its realistic, unglamorized picture of working-class life came partly from her own experience. Growing up as a Jewish outcast in the strict Mormon society of Salt Lake City, Utah, Roseanne had a difficult time. As a teenager in the 1960s, she had a terrifying, near-death experience and was placed in a mental institution. Becoming a mother at an early age, Roseanne was a member of the working poor and lived in a trailer park. But never giving up, she succeeded as a stand-up comedian in the 1980s and finally made a breakthrough into television, hosting several specials before starring in her own show, *Roseanne*, in 1988.

In her first autobiography, entitled *Roseanne: My Life as a Woman*, the popular actress vividly remembered her childbirth:

Nothing, nothing will ever be terrifying and grotesque as this. And then I feel a pressure that begins in my lower back and it reminds me of rice paper, tearing rice paper, so swift and easy and it comes apart. "It's a girl," they say, and my husband says, "Oh, honey, it's a girl." And she is screaming and I think of her terror, she has been squeezed alive for eight and one half hours, and her body has been forced through a passage tight around her head, a passage of human flesh and bone and blood, blood, blood.

And I take her into my arms while the doctor and my husband marvel at the meaning in all of this, and I hold her, knowing that she is terrified of my body and I am torn and terrified from her body, and the agony and power of motherhood now is clear to me.

Now I know why mothers love their children—because we have been one-in-hell together. Now it is all over, and I see the monster and she can feel the machine of my grinding, twisting body, now giving comfort, as I give her my breast and think: I am a woman giving birth to myself.

Cher

An actress, singer, and director, Cher (born Cherilyn LaPierre Sarkisian) has enjoyed huge popularity for more than thirty-five years. She met her first husband, Sonny Bono, a recording producer, in a coffee shop when she was sixteen. The two began performing together as a musical act, at one point billing themselves as "Caesar and Cleo." They married when Cher was eighteen, and by 1965, Sonny and Cher were a popular act, renowned on the West Coast for their outrageous outfits. Their first big hit single was "I Got You, Babe," which sold more than four million copies.

After starring in *The Sonny and Cher Comedy Hour* and then *The Sonny and Cher Show*, Cher did a stint on the Las Vegas circuit before launching a successful film career. She received a Best Supporting Actress Oscar nomination for her role in *Silkwood* and a Best Actress Academy Award for *Moonstruck*. Cher's other notable movies include *Mask, Suspect, Witches of Eastwick, Mermaids*, and *Tea with Mussolini*. In 1999, Cher's album *Believe*, containing the smash single of the same title, made her, at age fifty-two, the oldest American woman ever to record a number one hit. Since then, Cher's prolific performing career has included concert tours and TV appearances.

In her memoir, *The First Time, Cher*, the entertainer recalled her first live birth after suffering four miscarriages:

I got down to the hospital about six o'clock in the evening. On my way there, I noticed that the moon was huge and full—or was it the sun? I was so scared I couldn't tell. My knees were shaking, and my teeth were chattering. They put me in a wheelchair, and Son [Sonny] met me at the front entrance with Denis, our best friend and assistant, taking pictures of the whole thing. Son was going, "Sweetheart, later on you're really gonna like it that we have these pictures."

And I said, "Sonny, if you don't stop the picture-taking crap, I'm going to kill you."

By the time I got down to the delivery room, everything in my body was shaking. I felt better when my doctor and his nurse, Beth, arrived. She'd been my closest friend during the pregnancy. . . . People weren't doing natural childbirth in those days, and I certainly wanted to cut down the pain, but I'd also wanted to be conscious. . . .

I finally saw my daughter late that night. She was so cute, with great big eyes and so much black hair she looked like an Eskimo, and she was so tiny. And I thought, *What am I going to do? I don't know how to take care of her—I don't know anything.* I was so nervous that I took a sleeping pill, which didn't do anything at all, and I lay in bed sweating all night long.

We named her Chastity, after the movie I'd made with Sonny—it might have been a huge flop, but I'd always loved the name. For her middle name, I wanted to do something for Son, so I named her Chastity Son.

Elizabeth Barrett Browning

Elizabeth Barrett Browning was one of Victorian England's most famous poets, with works including the romantically passionate *Sonnets from the Portuguese*. During her lifetime, Elizabeth Barrett came to be more admired for her literary talent than her poet-husband, Robert Browning.

Educated at home in classical Greek, Latin, and several modern languages, Elizabeth Barrett showed early genius; and at the age of thirteen she published, with her father's financial assistance, a long poem. At the age of fifteen, she almost died from spinal injuries suffered in a fall—and remained a semi-invalid throughout her ensuing life. In 1845, when Barrett was nearly forty and well known in her own right, she met the poet Robert Browning and the two married the following year. In *The Immortal Lovers*, biographer Frances Linwar recounted:

As January of the new year went into February, Mrs. Browning drew near her term. The doctor was hopeful that all would go well, even though Mrs. Browning was forty-three and had a long history of illness. She had taken every precaution this time, and prayed that at last the hypothetical claimant whom she and Browning had discussed before their marriage would come to crown their happiness. . . . The claimant, "a fine, strong boy, like

Harry Gill with the voice of three," a voice indeed that made [Mr.] Browning aware of his existence through a thick wall and a double door, arrived at Casa Guidi on the 9th of March, 1849.

Mrs. Browning bore her twenty-one hours' pain without one cry or tear, and recovered with extraordinary speed. [Mr.] Browning was so overwhelmed by this latest of Ba's achievements that he lapsed into ungrammar in one of his letters broadcasting the news: "Ba is going on perfectly good. . . ." God, he went on, had rewarded that dearest, most precious of creatures for her patience, goodness, and self-denial. . . .

She now appeared in her little front caps of net with a worsted edge—Wilson's handiwork—the picture of blissful motherhood. "You never saw such fat, rosy, lively child," she boasted with a new pride. Henceforth, her letters never failed to contain some allusion to the beauty, the intelligence, the wonder of her little Florentine.

Agatha Christie

Agatha Christie, born in Devon, England, in 1890, was acclaimed as one of the greatest mystery writers of modern time. She was educated at home by her mother. While serving as a volunteer nurse during

World War I, she began actively writing and published her first novel soon after. In 1926, with the appearance of *The Murder of Roger Ackroyd*, Agatha gained major recognition. There followed seventy-five successful novels, twenty-five of them featuring the detective Hercule Poirot. *Witness for the Prosecution, Death on the Nile*, and *Murder on the Orient Express* were all adapted for film.

In *An Autobiography*, Christie recalled her pregnancy and labor:

It seemed to me, in my ignorance, that so much vomiting would have a bad effect on our coming child—that it would be starved. This, however, was far from the case. Although I continued to be sick up to the day of the birth, I had a strapping eight-and-a-half pound daughter, and I myself, though never seeming to retain any nourishment at all, had put on rather than lost weight.

The whole thing was like a nine-month ocean voyage to which you never got acclimatized. When Rosalind was born, and I found a doctor and a nurse leaning over me, the doctor saying, "Well, you've got a lovely daughter!" I responded with the important announcement: "I don't feel sick any more. How wonderful!"

Archie and I had great arguments the preceding month about names, and about which sex we wanted. Archie was very definite that he must have a daughter.

"I'm not going to have a boy," he said, "because I can see I should be jealous of it. I'd be jealous of your paying attention to it."

"But I should pay just as much attention to a girl!"

"No, it wouldn't be the same thing."

We argued about a name. Archie wanted Enid. I wanted Martha. He shifted to Elaine—I tried Harriet. Not till after she was born did we compromise on Rosalind.

Erica Jong

The author of fiction, essays, and poetry, Erica Jong remains best known for her racy novel *Fear of Flying*, published in 1973. For many at the time, it personified a new feminism celebrating sensuality and passion. A lifelong New Yorker, Jong continues to address such themes in her varied writing. Her witty memoir, *Fear of Fifty*, contains this reminiscence:

> Jonathan was not allowed into the Operating Room. I barely was myself. This was a sacred circle of medical men. A spinal block was administered and my legs grew numb. I could feel cutting but no pain.

A bloody lump was lifted high for me to see.

"Is that the placenta?" I asked.

"It's your daughter," said David, putting a little creature covered in iron-ore-colored blood into my arms. She was wearing a hastily wrapped pink blanket and fluttering her blood-caked lids. Her eyes of undersea blue met mine.

"Welcome, little stranger," I said, weeping and washing her face with my tears. . . .

She was mine and not-mine all at once. She was the most beautiful thing I had ever seen and the most terrifying. God had dropped into my life wearing Molly's face. Or else God's hostage. My life henceforth would not belong to me alone.

Grace Slick

Grace Slick was the original "great rock diva." As the lead singer of Jefferson Airplane, which produced classics like "White Rabbit" and "Somebody to Love," she was at the forefront of the 1960s and '70s counterculture. As one of the first female rock stars (as opposed to pop singers), Grace helped redefine women's role in modern music, though, ironically, she was neither an original member of Jefferson Airplane nor with the band at the very end. In *Somebody to Love?: A Rock and Roll Memoir*, Slick recalled the birth of her daughter, named China:

I'd previously told my doctor that when I was ready to give birth, I wanted an anaesthetic to administer copious amounts of whatever they had in stock to kill the pain. But the anesthetist never showed up. In the spaces between the contractions that were turning me into a rictus-faced gargoyle, I inquired as to the whereabouts of the missing dispenser.

"Oh, he isn't here yet," the various nurses informed me, something they continued to say all night long. I hadn't taken any Lamaze or Lamodge or whatever-it-is classes, because no mater what kind of cute tiny breaths you practice, I figured that in the final analysis, you've got a mass the size of a cantaloupe coming out of a hole the size of a fifty-cent piece.

That simple bit of physics means PAIN.

I told myself that women had been doing this thing called childbirth forever. Don't worry about it, I kept thinking. Remember that it's only a few hours of hideous groaning and then you have a whole new person to love. So I had my daughter by natural childbirth, an accidental route I'd definitely not chosen.

I'd been warned that newborns do not look like the Gerber baby. They said "it" would probably be a blood-covered, squalling, blue-faced, wrinkled mess, so I was ready for a remnant of some atomic mishap. But she was a lovely, smooth-skinned, pink-and-white being, content just to lie there and be cuddled and admired by her mother.

Barbra Streisand

Streisand may have enjoyed her pregnancy, but as James Spada's biography reveals, she found labor a very different affair:

As the baby's delivery approached, Elliott helped Barbra every morning with her breathing exercises in anticipation of the natural delivery. Barbra turned her cluttered sewing room into a temporary nursery, with a violet-colored tile floor and pointillist wallpaper. She picked out matching fabric and painted the accessories herself.

Once everything was ready, all that remained to do was wait. And wait. And wait. Although she expected the baby around December 20, Barbra didn't go into labor—despite two false alarms—until six in the morning on Thursday, December 29. Certain within two hours that this was the real thing, Barbra checked into Mount Sinai Hospital at nine. Nearly six more hours of labor followed. "It was very traumatic," Elliott said, "but Barbra was very brave. We held hands and talked about a son or daughter."

When her doctor discovered the baby was in the breech position (feet first) inside Barbra's womb, they decided that a caesarian section would be necessary to avoid any possible damage to the child during delivery. The incision, of course. . . . dashed her hope of experiencing a natural birth, and she was unconscious when the baby, a healthy seven-pound, three-ounce boy, made his entrance into the world at 2:55 P.M.

When Jason Emanuel Gould was brought to his mother in room 507—with the name Angelina Scarangella on the door— she could barely trust her eyes. "I could not believe he grew inside of me." She held the child with trepidation and awe, feeling more love flow from within her than she ever had before. . . .

Having a boy child, Barbra [later said,] taught her a great deal about men. "You realize that they are these little people, and they want to be held, and they cry, and they get hurt, just like women. Unfortunately society has put these pressures on men to be *strong*, and it's quite unfair. It's nice to find a man who's as vulnerable as he is strong."

Expressing Fatherly Affection

Kevin Costner

Actor, producer, and director Kevin Costner is best known for his epic Western film *Dances with Wolves*, which won Academy Awards in 1990 for both Best Picture and Best Director, as well as acclaim for Costner's acting. He grew up in southern California, and as a teenager decided on an acting career. Joining a community theater group while still in college, Costner broke into film with the straight-to-video *Sizzle Beach, U.S.A.*, with a "hunk" role he immediately regretted; but he advanced his career effectively in such films as *Silverado, The Untouchables*, and *No Way Out*. Though Costner has had several box-office flops, his well-received movies have included *Bull Durham, Field of Dreams, Message in a Bottle, For Love of the Game*, and *Thirteen Days*.

The father of four, Costner observed in an interview for *Redbook*:

It's important to tell someone how beautiful they look and what they mean to you on a daily basis. I tell my children every day that I love them—sometimes four or five times in a day. It doesn't preclude me from disciplining them. But when I kiss them good night or I talk to them on the phone, the last thing we tell each other is how much we love and miss each other.

My dad played with me and held me, and I remember one of my favorite things now—which I didn't like at first—was when he'd get tired and he'd say, "Let's take a nap. I want to take a nap, and I need you to lie down too." I realize he wanted me to lie down because otherwise I would make so much noise. Now I take naps, and I love it when my kids lie down with me and take a nap. But Mom was the demonstrative one in our family, the one who would talk to us about love, about what it meant.

Expressing Fatherly Pride

Bronson Alcott

Bronson Alcott was a prominent New England philosopher and social reformer of the mid-nineteenth century. His notable friends included Ralph Waldo Emerson, Margaret Fuller, and Henry David Thoreau. Alcott is also famous as the father of Louisa May Alcott, who wrote *Little Women* and other popular novels. He created the Temple School in Boston, which is devoted to spiritual development, and also helped found several utopian communes.

In a November 1832 letter to his mother, Alcott wrote joyfully about his newborn, Louisa May, and her toddler sister Anna:

Besides reflections on my life and experience [today], this is *the birth of a second daughter on my own birthday.* She is a very fine, fat little creature, much larger than Anna was at birth, with a firm constitution for building up a fine character—which, I trust, we shall do our part to accomplish.

Little Anna, now twenty months old, is remarkably well, active, and intelligent. She has passed through the usual complaints of children during the first year or eighteen months of life, and has a large stock of health and strength for future trials. Her heart and mind develop beautifully—she is full of affection and intelligence—of freshness and activity, and begins to talk a few words intelligibly. We think she has her mother's heart and her father's mind; time will tell.

Fatherhood Is a Sacred Bond

Paul Palnik

Paul Palnik is an artist based in Columbus, Ohio, whose posters and cartoons are infused with a warm spirituality drawing on biblical images and themes. The author of *Couples* and *The Palnik Poster Book*, he lectures widely on creativity and is currently artistic consultant to the Jewish Theological Seminary in New York City and its branch in Israel. As the father of four, Palnik offered this reminiscence about the birth of his son, Eli, in Jerusalem:

Standing in the baby birthing room at Hadassah Hospital in Jerusalem, the doctor handed me my newborn son. The little fellow had just entered our raucous world from the quiet, dark comfort of his mother's warm womb. In Israel, the child is handed to the father even before the infant is laid upon the mother's breast to suckle. As is the custom among many Jews, it was my privilege to open my son's tightly closed eyes with my fingers.

Looking down at his tiny face, my heart and soul consumed me with the most exquisite sense of the wondrous mystery of profound life I had ever experienced. My hands are huge and clumsy, but somehow my thick fingers were granted the ability to move with a gentle grace and a delicate touch as I opened his tiny eyelids. Immediately he began looking about, and I could see that he was trying to focus his never-before-used eyes on me. My eyes looked deeply into his and I was transformed: no longer the human being that I had always been. We named our son Eli, which means in Hebrew, "My God." His blessing shines in my life to this very moment and my gratitude will be with me forever.

Fostering Creativity

Jacqueline Kennedy Onassis

When Jacqueline "Jackie" Kennedy Onassis died shortly before her sixty-fifth birthday, she left behind an unforgettable legacy. Certainly, Jackie was admired for her accomplishments as an influential book editor and tireless national spokesperson for the arts in the United States. She is probably best remembered, however, for her quiet dignity as a bereaved widow to her family—and the entire, stunned nation—in the aftermath of President John F. Kennedy's assassination in 1963. Raising her two children, Caroline and John, to maturity was a challenging venture for Jackie. She once said, "The things you do with your children, you never forget."

Jackie often emphasized the importance of nurturing imagination and creativity when asked about her child-rearing philosophy:

Perhaps some painting—just some splattering of watercolors or crayon lines the way a child loves to do it—is the first step. Whenever I paint now, I put up a child's paint box for Caroline beside me. She really prefers to dip the brushes in water, smear the paints, and make a mess, but it is a treat for her to paint with her mother.

Perhaps this will develop a latent talent; perhaps it will merely do what it did for me, produce occasional paintings which only one's family could admire, and be a source of pleasure and relaxation.

When I was a child, my mother helped us enormously with our creative instincts. She interested us in languages, poetry, and art as young children. She encouraged us to make things for birthday presents instead of buying them. So perhaps we would paint a picture or write a poem or memorize something.

When I was ten years old, I memorized *The Vision of Sir Launfal* by James Russell Lowell for my mother's birthday. It was eleven pages long in my poetry book and I was enormously proud of myself at the time. I can still remember whole passages of it today.

I mention these examples to show that a mind, trained young to retain, continues to do so.

On another occasion, the celebrated First Lady observed:

People have too many theories about child-rearing. I believe simply in love, security, and discipline.

Gaining Identical Twins

Michael J. Fox

Too small at five feet, four inches to pursue his childhood dream of professional hockey, Canadian-born Michael J. Fox wisely chose an acting career instead, and he debuted on TV at the age of fifteen. With seven years on the popular TV show *Family Ties*, he developed a persona of boyish charm blended with impeccable comic acting. Among Fox's most popular films are the *Back to the Future* trilogy, *The Secret of My Success, Stuart Little*, and *Stuart Little 2*, in which he contributed his trademark voice and comic flair as the title character—a little white mouse—in film adaptations of E.B. White's children's novel.

In recent years, Fox has gained prominence for his award-winning performance on ABC's TV show *Spin City*, as well as his activism for curative research on Parkinson's disease, an illness with which he has been struggling since the age of thirty. Now the father of four with wife Tracy Pollan, Fox recalled in *Lucky Man: A Memoir*:

At the end of the second week in February, I left the movie set in California and boarded a plane for New York. The babies weren't due until March, but, as Tracy's obstetrician told us, "It's easier to get two Volkswagons out of a garage than two Buicks," so he recommended inducing birth a month early. We still had no idea about the sex of the babies, but we did know from the amnio that they were identical. So, whatever they were, boys or girls, Tracy would be delivering a matched set.

On February 15, 1995, we met our twin daughters. The first born was tiny and as white as alabaster, and the second, eight minutes younger, was a pound heavier and a lurid purple color. Something called twin-to-twin transfusions had been happening *in utero*, whereby one twin had been nearly monopolizing the blood supply. Happily, in a matter of weeks after delivery, the two girls were equally healthy.

We named the smaller, older baby Aquinnah, the Wampenoag Indian name for the town in Martha's Vineyard where we'd spent many summers. We wanted a colorful name for this pale, delicate little creature, and Aquinnah, according to one translation, literally means "beautiful colors by the sea." The younger girl we called Schyler, a Dutch name meaning scholar, or teacher.

I had been learning something important about life over the course of this year of miracles, and the birth of the twins brought the teaching all the way home. During the long, agonizing period following my diagnosis, when Tracy, for reasons that are obvious to me now, was reluctant to consider adding to our family, I had grown bitter from regret. . . .

Now we'd been given two beautiful infant daughters. This was the lesson: it wasn't for me to fret about time or loss, but to appreciate each day, move forward, and have faith that something larger was at work, something with its own sense of timing and balance.

Gaining Inspiration from Your Baby

Martin Luther King Jr.

Martin Luther King Jr. was the most important civil rights leader of modern time. Raised in Montgomery, Alabama, and ordained as a minister in 1957, King was a charismatic speaker, tireless organizer, and inspiring activist. His momentous "I have a dream" speech, delivered before hundreds of thousands of supporters at the 1963 March on Washington, was a turning point in U.S. history. At the time of his assassination at age thirty-eight in 1968, King was already seeking to build a broader national and international agenda for justice and world peace. His wife reminisced:

> During my pregnancy, Martin was very attentive and concerned. We were both a little anxious for fear something would go wrong, but I suppose you always have these anxieties about the first one, especially when the child is wanted so much. Martin

wanted a boy first. He always referred to the unborn baby as his son. "My son," he would say, "I want my son to be named Martin Luther King III."

In November, I went to St. Jude's Hospital to have my baby. It was a Catholic hospital, of course, and was unusual because it was the only hospital in Montgomery where Negroes could be treated decently. Then, though normally St. Jude's kept whites and blacks separated, if the hospital became overcrowded, they would be put together, particularly in the maternity ward.

Our baby was born on November 17, 1954. She was a big healthy girl weighing nine pounds, eleven and one half ounces. It turned out, as it usually does, that Martin did not mind at all not having a son. She was such a lovable child; she was very close to his heart. . . .

Martin always said that Yoki came at a time in his life when he needed something to take his mind off the tremendous pressures that bore down upon him. When he came home from the stress and turmoil that he was suddenly plunged into, the baby was there cooing and cuddly and trustful and loving. There is something renewing about a small child—something he needed very much, because less than three weeks after Yoki was born, a seamstress named Rosa Parks refused to give up her seat on a Montgomery bus, and the Movement was born.

Getting Grandmotherly Help

Hank Aaron

"Hammerin' Hank" Aaron earned his nickname by clubbing 755 round-trippers over his twenty-three-year career. Not only did he raise the bar for home runs, but he also established twelve other major league career records, including most games, at-bats, total bases, and runs-batted-in. Aaron usually played the infield, but also gained recognition as an excellent outfielder, winning three Golden Glove awards. He earned National League Most Valuable Player honors in 1957, and appeared in a record twenty-four All Star games. A quiet and effective leader, Aaron is now an executive with the Braves.

In his autobiography, *I Had a Hammer*, Aaron recalled:

This winter, nine months after Hankie was born, Barbara gave birth to our third and fourth children, twin boys we named Gary and Larry. They were born prematurely, and Gary never made it out of the hospital. Larry was very weak, and after a few months the reports from the doctors weren't encouraging. Mama still thought about my brother Alfred dying of pneumonia, and she did all she could to keep Larry out of the weather.

We took him to Mobile [Alabama] to stay with Mama. As soon as he got there, she bathed him and bundled him up and then fed him, and it was the best he had ever eaten in his life. Then he went to sleep, and from that moment on, he started to improve. I have no doubt that Mama saved that boy's life. He stayed with her while he was growing up.

He wore a stocking cap all the time, and she even had him ride his bicycle in the house. Larry had problems with epilepsy, but Mama feeding him greens and keeping him warm and giving him his medication, he grew up strong.

Getting to Know Your Newborn

Maya Angelou

When Maya Angelou read her newest poem at former President Bill Clinton's 1993 inauguration, it was another landmark achievement in her multifaceted career. The author of numerous magazine articles and more than ten books, including *I Know Why the Caged Bird Sings, I Shall Not Be Moved*, and *Now Sheba Sings the Song*, Angelou has earned both Pulitzer Prize and National Book Award nominations.

Maya was the second child and only daughter of urban African American parents. She was sent, along with her brother, Bailey, to be raised by her paternal grandmother—a storekeeper in Stamps, Arkansas. Working with Dr. Martin Luther King Jr. during the 1960s, Angelou has since gained acclaim as an actress, playwright, and director, and has made hundreds of television appearances. She also teaches American Studies at Wake Forest University in North Carolina.

In her memoir *I Know Why the Caged Bird Sings*, Angelou related:

After a short labor, and without too much pain (I decided that the pain of delivery was overrated), my son was born. Just as gratefulness was confused in my mind with love, so possession became mixed up with motherhood. I had a baby. He was beautiful and mine. Totally mine. No one had bought him for me. No one had helped me endure the sickly gray months. I had had help in the child's conception, but no one could deny that I had an immaculate pregnancy.

Totally my possession, and I was afraid to touch him. Home from the hospital, I sat for hours by his bassinet and absorbed his mysterious perfection. His extremities were so dainty they appeared unfinished. Mother handled him easily with the casual confidence of a baby nurse, but I dreaded being forced to change his diapers. Wasn't I famous for awkwardness? Suppose I let him slip, or put my fingers on that throbbing pulse on the top of his head?

Mother came to my bed one night bringing my three-week-old baby. She pulled the cover back and told me to get up and hold him while she put rubber sheets on my bed. She explained that he was going to sleep with me.

I begged in vain. I was sure to roll over and crush out his life or break those fragile bones. She wouldn't hear of it, and within minutes the pretty golden baby was lying on his back in the center of my bed, laughing at me.

I lay on the edge of the bed, stiff with fear, and vowed not to sleep all night long. But the eat-sleep routine I had begun in the hospital, and kept up under Mother's dictatorial command, got the better of me. I dropped off.

My shoulder was shaken gently. Mother whispered, "Maya, wake up. But don't move."

I knew immediately that the wakening had to do with the baby. I tensed. "I'm awake."

She turned the light on and said, "Look at the baby." My fears were so powerful I couldn't move to look at the center of the bed. She said again, "Look at the baby." I didn't hear sadness in her voice, and that helped me to break the bonds of terror. The baby was no longer in the center of the bed. At first I thought he had moved. But after closer investigation, I found that I was lying on my stomach with my arm bent at a right angle. Under the tent of blanket, which was poled by my elbow and forearm, the baby slept touching my side. Mother whispered, "See, you don't have to think about doing the right thing. If you're for the right thing, then you do it without thinking."

She turned out the light and I patted my son's body lightly and went back to sleep.

Getting Toys for Your Child

Mary Todd Lincoln

Mary Todd was, from all historical evidence, the first and only love of Abraham Lincoln. High-spirited, quick-witted, and well-educated, she came from a distinguished Kentucky family, and her Springfield, Illinois relatives belonged to the social aristocracy of the town. Some of them frowned on her association with the lower-echelon Lincoln, and occasionally, he, too, had doubts whether he could ever make her happy. But they became engaged, and then married in November 1842.

Mary Todd Lincoln's life was marked by personal tragedy. Besides witnessing her husband's assassination by her side in 1865, she suffered the deaths of three of their four sons; only Robert, the eldest, survived to adulthood. On leaving the White House as First Lady, Mary was both a mental and physical wreck. Years of subsequent travel failed to restore her well-being, and she was briefly committed to a private sanitarium in 1875, before eventually going to live with her sister.

In May 1860, Mary penned this maternal letter to a prominent anti-slavery Kansas publisher who had stopped in Springfield with two convention flags, and inadvertently took both away with him:

Dear Sir:

One of my boys appears to claim prior possession of the smallest flag and is inconsolable for its absence. I believe it is too small to do you any service, and as he is so urgent to have it again, and as I am sure the largest one will be quite sufficient, I will ask you to send it to us the first opportunity you may have.

It is especially as he claims it, and I feel it is as necessary to keep one's word with a child as with a grown person.

Giving Birth to Twins

Madeleine Albright

Nominated by President Clinton in 1996, Madeleine Albright was the first woman to be U.S. secretary of state. Prior to her appointment, she served as the U.S. permanent representative to the United Nations and as a member of the U.S. National Security Council. Emigrating as a child with her family from Poland on the eve of World War II, Albright earned her doctorate in public law and government from Columbia University and taught courses on Eastern European affairs at Georgetown University. In *Seasons of Her Life*, biographer Ann Blackman recounted:

> Madeleine was pregnant. As she grew larger and larger, she began walking as a way to lose weight. She would walk five miles, stop for a cup of coffee, then turn around and walk home. She also started drinking a liquid diet meal popular at the time

called Metracal. One day, walking to her doctor's office in the next town, she spotted a sign advertising Russian lessons at Hofstra University in nearby Hempstead, New York.

Madeleine had always wanted to learn Russian. . . . The eighthour-a-day Hofstra classes began in June and lasted eight weeks. The baby was due the first week in August. Madeleine calculated that if she started the course, she might not be able to finish it.

"Too bad I can't do that," she thought as she walked to the doctor's office one day. When she arrived, the physician examined her. "I think you are having at least two," he said. Walking home, Madeleine contemplated what this new twist in her life would entail.

Six weeks later, June 17, 1961, Madeleine gave birth to twins. Anne was named after Madeleine's mother, whose official name was Anna; Alice after her great-aunt Alicia Patterson. The girls were six weeks premature. Anne weighed three pounds, six ounces; Alice, three pounds, eight ounces.

The doctor told the Albrights that if the babies did not reinflate their lungs within forty-eight hours, they would not survive. If they did live, they could not leave the hospital until they weighed five pounds. Because they were extremely vulnerable to infection, even their mother was not allowed to touch them.

"I was twenty-four years old and terrified," Madeleine Albright [recalled]. There was nothing I could do. My husband was working. I didn't have a job. I couldn't go and [be with] my children. All I could do was look at them through the glass."

To distract herself, Albright signed up for the Russian language class she had been thinking about earlier. "It occupied me," she reminisced. "I'd go every morning." When her father took advantage of a university lecture and came East in July to see his first grandchildren, Madeleine greeted him in Russian.

Jane Seymour

Jane Seymour began performing as a professional London ballet dancer before knee injuries caused her to shift her interest to acting. She is best known for her made-for-TV dramas, with more than fifty films and TV programs to her credit, including the long-running CBS hit *Dr. Quinn, Medicine Woman*. The movie *Somewhere in Time*, in which she co-starred with Christopher Reeve, has become a cult classic for its imaginative romantic passion. Over the years, Seymour has won a series of Emmy nominations. She and her husband, the Hollywood producer, director, and actor James Keach, together have raised six children, including twins Kris and John. In her parenting guidebook, *Two at a Time*, Seymour reflected on an enticing aspect of giving birth to twins when she was forty-six years old:

One of the many great sidelights about having twins is choosing their names. You get to use not one, but two of your favorite names—four if you're into middle names. In some families, it can be a real group project just coming up with that many favorites. In our family, it was just James and I who chose the names.

Actually, we settled on their names very quickly, early in the pregnancy. There was no searching and sifting through dozens of candidates. But strangely enough, the names they ended up with weren't exactly the ones we chose. We knew first of all that we wanted to name one John, after my father and after Johnny Cash, with whom we'd become good friends after he made several guest appearances on *Dr. Quinn*. We also knew that we wanted the name Kristopher after my friend Christopher Reeve, but with a K instead of a C because we liked how that went with Keach. . . .

Everyone seems to have a story about naming their twins. It *is* an important step in your babies' lives. If you have had a pregnancy like most women who have had twins, you will have seen your babies via ultrasound many times before they are born. Like James and I, you may also have watched your babies' personalities evolve in utero, so you might have some idea which baby will be named what before they are born. . . .

So while certain aspects of naming your babies may be out of your control, I can only urge you to choose names that have meaning for you. But I would also urge you to think of the babies who will carry them, and of their circumstances as twins. Names that seem cute on infants can seem anything but cute on adults.

Cybill Shepherd

Few women in the past thirty years have ignited the American imagination like Cybill Shepherd. Born and raised in Memphis, in 1968 she won "Model of the Year" from Stewart Models and appeared on the covers of *Glamour, Life, People*, and *Vogue*, among others. In 1971, she made her film debut in the highly acclaimed *The Last Picture Show*, which led to starring roles in such films as *The Heartbreak Kid, Taxi Driver, Daisy Miller, Married to It*, and *Chances Are*. Shepherd's performing career has included theatrical productions, TV shows (including her self-named sitcom), and hosting of the Emmy and Golden Globe Awards, and, most recently, of the talk show *Men Are from Mars, Women Are from Venus*, inspired by John Gray's best-seller of the same name.

In her memoir *Cybill Disobedience*, the actress reminisced:

I was getting dressed for the Golden Globe Awards, and my dress didn't fit. There was no mistaking the reason. The stomach pooches out more quickly in a second pregnancy because the muscles have been pregnant before. By the time I scheduled a doctor's appointment, a test was a formality—I was so violently nauseated I couldn't eat.

When the obstetrician got the results back from the lab, she called me. "Either you're further along in your pregnancy than you thought," she said, "or you're having twins."

I dismissed this possibility, even though my grandmother's sister and their grandmother had had twins. . . .

By my third trimester, I was so huge I began to resemble Marlon Brando. I could no longer get off my futon on the floor, so I had to crawl to the edge and then push myself up. One early morning, I was awakened by an earthquake, and in terror, I stood straight up and jumped off the platform, running to see if [eight-year-old] Clementine was all right. She was, but . . . I felt like I was walking around carrying two bowling balls between my legs. Every night I prayed, "Please God, let me get over this pain before I go into labor."

A few weeks before my due date . . . Molly Ariel and Cyrus Zachariah were born thirteen hours [after my water broke], both named for their great-grandparents but known by their middle names. Those thirteen hours were harrowing. I began begging for drugs and screaming, "Kill me! Kill me! Cut the babies out!"

A few moments later, before any drugs could be given, Ariel was born followed by Zachariah.

About her first child, Shepherd has also commented,

> Watching Clementine grow is one of the great satisfactions of my life. The center of the universe shifting from myself to another person is a great relief. It gives me the chance to give to another person. I'm not so concerned about my own life as I was before.

Margaret Thatcher

Margaret Thatcher was the first woman to serve as England's prime minister. Born into a middle-class, politically involved family in Linconshire, she studied at Oxford University, worked as a research chemist after World War II, and then shifted to a career in law and politics while raising two children. She became the Conservative Party leader and prime minister in 1975 and for fifteen years politically headed her nation; her three-term tenure marked her as England's longest-serving prime minister in the twentieth century.

Ten years after resigning her post due to party infighting about her stringent economic policies, Thatcher was made a life peer by England's royalty. She continues to advance her political views through public speaking, writing, and a private foundation named for her. In her autobiography, *The Path to Power*, Thatcher reminisced about an important phase of her womanhood:

The question which John Hare had raised with me about how I would combine my home life with politics was soon to become even more sensitive. For in August 1953 the twins, Mark and Carol, put in an appearance. Late one Thursday night, some six weeks before what we still called "the baby" was due, I began to have pains.

I had seen the doctor that day and he asked me to come back on the Monday for an X-ray because there was something he wanted to check. Now Monday seemed a very long way away, and off I was immediately taken to the hospital. I was given a sedative which helped me sleep through the night. Then on Friday the X-ray was taken and to the great surprise of all it was discovered that I was to be the mother of twins.

Unfortunately, that's not the whole story. The situation required a Caesarian operation the following day. The two tiny babies—a boy and a girl—had to wait a little before they saw their father. For Denis, imagining that all was progressing smoothly, had very sensibly gone to the Oval to watch the Test

Match and it proved quite impossible to contact him. On that day, he received two pieces of good but equally surprising news: England won the Ashes, and he found himself the proud father of twins.

The pull of a mother toward her children is perhaps the strongest and most instinctive emotion we have. I was never one of those people who regarded being "just" a mother or indeed "just" a housewife as second best. Indeed, whenever I heard such implicit assumptions made both before and after I became Prime Minister, it would make me very angry indeed. Of course, I knew that being a mother was a vocation of a very high kind.

Help from the Baby's Siblings

Katharine Graham

The daughter of a Wall Street tycoon and a Washington power broker, the late Katharine Graham was raised by one of the most politically influential families of the twentieth century. From the day her father bought the *Washington Post* in 1933, her life was marked, and sometimes scarred, by the ups and downs of politics in Washington, D.C. After her husband Phil Graham's suicide in 1963, Katherine was suddenly faced with publishing the *Post* herself. Despite an awkward start, she went on to publish the *Pentagon Papers* and allow reporters Woodward and Bernstein to crack open the Watergate scandal that led to President Nixon's resignation.

Up to her sudden death from a fall in 2001, Graham was a best-selling author, preeminent Capitol Hill hostess, and, according to some Washington insiders, among the most powerful women in the world. As Katharine Graham recounted about young motherhood in her memoir, *Personal History:*

At times, Donny was a difficult baby. He took a great deal of patience, and I had little. From the age of six months to a year, he alternated between violent activity and ensuing exhaustion and crankiness. It was often hard to get him to eat.

One day, when he had thrown his entire dinner on the floor, I was so desperate that I asked Lally [his older sister] what to do. With total common sense, she suggested, "Try him with a sandwich." I must say it worked quite well. After that, she became my able and enthusiastic assistant.

Honoring Your Roots

Roxanne Swentzell

Born into a family of potters and a tribe famed for ceramics—the Santa Clara Pueblo Indians—it was only natural that Roxanne Swentzell grew up to become a professional artist working with clay. "I'm a mud person," she quips. Raised in Santa Fe, New Mexico, she also trained there, at the Institute of American Indian Arts, and at the Portland Museum Art School as well. Specializing in creating clay figures alone or in family groupings, Swentzell has won many awards and lives in the Santa Clara Pueblo. Among her popular works is "Emergence of the Clowns," which toured the United States, Canada, and New Zealand and showed at the White House. In the anthology *A Question of Balance*, Swentzell observed:

> The whole Pueblo world was concerned with keeping things in balance: keeping themselves in balance with nature, keeping

themselves in balance with their female and male sides. If you were a man and you were called a mother or a woman, you were being told something very good about yourself. You were a whole person, you were a much bigger person than just a man.

They really honored the female. The earth, being the mother, was continuously being remembered in the dances, in the kivas, in the ceremonies. The clowns came out of the mother, the earth; they were the first into this level of the world. That sculpture was trying to get people to remember: we're from this earth, we are creatures of this earth, she is our mother.

Remember where you came from. She is the one who gives you life, and if you destroy her, then you destroy yourself. In Pueblo culture, what makes you strong is your connections and your interdepedence.

Journaling Your Baby's Birth

Bronson Alcott

Like many philosophers and writers, New Englander Bronson Alcott regularly kept a journal. In November 1832, he celebrated the birth of his second daughter, Louisa May Alcott:

At this hour a child was born to us. This is a new and interesting event in the history of our lives. How delightful were the emotions produced by the first sounds of the infant's cry, making it seem that I was, indeed, a father! Joy, gratitude, hope, and affection were all mingled in our feeling.

As agents of the Supreme Parent, may we guide it in the paths of truth, duty, and happiness. May the divine blessing rest upon it. May its mind be the depository of everything pure, beautiful, and good [and] its heart of all sweet and tender affections.

Ralph Waldo Emerson

Like his older friend Bronson Alcott, Ralph Waldo Emerson was a devoted father as well as a visionary thinker. In 1839, he had already sired a son, Waldo, when composing this happy journal entry:

Yesterday morning, 24 February at 8 o'clock a daughter was born to me—a soft, quiet, swarthy little creature, apparently perfect and healthy. My second child. Blessings on thy head, little winter bud! Comest thou to try thy luck in this world and know if the things of God are things for thee? Well-assured and very soft and still, the little maiden expresses great contentment with all she finds, and [I see] her delicate but fixed determination to stay where she is, and grow.

So be it, my fair child! Lidian, who magnanimously makes my gods her gods, calls the babe Ellen. I can hardly ask more for thee, my babe, than that name implies. Be that vision and remain with us, and after us.

Keeping Memories Alive

Alicia Ostriker

A poet and literary critic, Alicia Ostriker is the author of more than a dozen books exploring feminine experience, including motherhood. "I started writing about [it] almost as soon as I became a mother," she reminisced in Judith Rosenberg's anthology, *A Question of Balance*. A professor of English at Rutgers University, Ostriker has been nominated for the National Book Award and written poetry books including *Songs, a Dream of Springtime, The Little Space*, and *The Mother/ Child Papers*, and such literary criticism as *The Nakedness of the Fathers: Biblical Visions and Revisions*.

> One of my great regrets is that I didn't write down more. You think you'll remember everything, and then you forget. [It's] helpful to keep journals and use tape recorders, cameras, and video to capture those fleeting moments. And don't be afraid to be honest. . . .

Having children keeps you real, keeps you open and on your toes, and is a continuing learning experience. [It] gives your mind and your passions a constant workout—which, if you want to keep them alive, is not a bad thing to have happen.

Learning the Importance of Faith

Jane Seymour

In her parenting guidebook, *Two at a Time*, Seymour highlighted not only the experience of having twins, but also the larger lessons that motherhood has taught her:

Looking back on the pregnancy and boys' birth, I'm struck by the mind-boggling array of lessons to be learned from the experience. Perhaps one of the biggest lessons for me was that I had the opportunity to gain a greater understanding of what I could control and what I could not. In our many failed attempts to get pregnant, James and I both did everything in our power to create the environment that would produce a pregnancy, and then we had to sit back and take what came—and it wasn't always what we'd wanted so badly. The same was true again when the boys were born. And again when we returned to the hospital with them. Now I see that each was a distinct opportunity to understand how little control we really have over the outcome of things!

The basic lack of control over the outcome of things we do, or over things our children do, means to me that it takes great faith to have children, and to raise them. Faith that we will learn as we go along, faith in our ability to live with a heart that's newly tender with love for these babies, and faith that we can bear to harbor that tiny spark of fear we hold for the well-being of those dearest to us.

Having the faith to take a deep breath, open our eyes and plunge ahead caring for our babies with all the confidence we can muster, as if we knew what we were doing—now that's a real gift.

I hope you'll be patient with yourself and with each other as you learn how to handle that gift, and the precious cargo you now hold in your arms.

Learning to be A Mother

Eleanor Roosevelt

Eleanor Roosevelt was admired not merely as the wife of President Franklin D. Roosevelt during America's darkest period, but also as a distinguished public figure in her own right. She was probably the most active First Lady in U.S. history, and served as a delegate to the newly formed United Nations after World War II and chairperson of its Human Rights Commission.

A later role model for women as a lecturer, writer, and social activist, Eleanor had little early child care experience. In her first memoir, *This Is My Story*, she recalled:

On May 3, 1906, my first child, a girl whom we named Anna Eleanor after my mother and myself, was born. The trained nurse who was with me was a very lovely person, Blanche Spring, and for many years she played an important part in my life, and I was always very deeply attached to her. She was not very well this first spring when she came to me, but she took care of me and of the baby single-handed. She adored babies, and she tried to teach me something about their care.

I had never had any interest in dolls or in little children, and I knew absolutely nothing about handling or feeding a baby. I acquired a young and inexperienced baby's nurse from the Babies Hospital. She knew a considerable amount about babies' diseases, but her inexperience made this knowledge almost a menace, for she was constantly looking for obscure illnesses and never expected that a well fed and well cared for baby would move along in a normal manner.

Marveling at Your Baby

Samuel Coleridge

A leading philosopher-poet of the nineteenth-century English romantic movement, Coleridge wrote such enduring works as "The Rime of the Ancient Mariner" and "Kubla Khan." Like his early friend William Wordsworth, Coleridge espoused a mystical outlook on life. While in his mid-twenties, he penned these famous words in the poem "Frost at Midnight," to his toddler son Hartley:

> Dear Babe, that sleepest cradled by my side,
> Whose gentle breathings heard in this deep calm,
> Fill up the interspersed vacancies
> And momentary pauses of the thought!
> My babe so beautiful! it thrills my heart
> With tender gladness, thus to look at thee,
> And think that thou shalt learn far other lore,

And in far other scenes! For I was reared
In the great city, pent 'mid cloisters dim,
And saw nought lovely but the sky and stars.
But *thou*, my babe! Shalt wander like a breeze
By lakes and sandy shores, beneath the crags
Of ancient mountain, and beneath the clouds,
Which image in their bulk both lakes and shores
And mountain crags; so shalt thou see and hear
The lovely shapes and sounds intelligible
Of that eternal language, which thy God
Utters from eternity doth teach
Himself in all, and all things in himself.
Great universal Teacher! he shall mould
Thy spirit, and by giving make it ask.

Meeting Your Newborn

Rebekah Baines Johnson

Lyndon Johnson, the thirty-sixth president of the United States, grew up in small-town Texas. His father was initially a successful and much-admired state politician, but the family sank into near poverty in the mid-1920s because of poor business conditions. As the oldest of five children, Lyndon was active and bright, but resisted studying. It was his culturally oriented mother, Rebekah, who read him stories from the Bible, history, and mythology, and taught him the alphabet at the age of two.

As a Johnson biographer related, "In the opinion of many people who observed their interaction over the years, Rebekah had an extraordinary hold on Lyndon; she imbued him with the belief that he could do anything, that nothing was too hard for him, and Lyndon reciprocated the feeling. He once told another interviewer, 'I think except for her I might not have made it through high school and certainly not through college. . . . She was a constant, dogged, determined influence on my life.'"

The evidence of her impact on Lyndon is even more striking from the words they exchanged when he was an adolescent and a man. "You can't realize the difference in the atmosphere after one of your sweet letters," he wrote her early in his college career. "Your letters always give me more strength, renewed courage, and that bulldog tenacity so essential to the success of any man," he wrote at the age of twenty-one.

"I love; I believe in you; I expect great things of you," Rebekah wrote her son when he was twenty-nine. "You have always justified my expectations, my hopes, my dreams. How dear to me you are, my darling boy, my devoted son, my strength and comfort."

As cited in Bill Adler's anthology *Motherhood: A Celebration*, Rebekah Johnson recalled her famous son's entrance into the world:

It was daybreak, Thursday, August 27, 1908, on the Sam Johnson farm on the Pedernales River, near Stonewall, Gillespie County. In the rambling old farmhouse of the young Sam Johnsons, lamps had burned all night. Now the light came in from the east, bringing a deep stillness, a stillness so profound and pervasive that it seemed as if the earth itself were listening.

And then there came a sharp compelling cry—the most awesome, happiest sound known to human ears—the cry of a newborn baby; the first child of Sam and Rebekah Johnson was "discovering America."

Sophia Loren

Sophia Loren was among the first foreign-language stars ever to attain international acclaim comparable with America's most popular domestic talents. Raised solely by her mother in war-torn Italy, Sophia (born Sophia Scicolone) worked as a print model in her early teens and participated in local beauty contests. In 1949, at the age of fifteen, she caught the attention of Italian producer Carlo Ponti while competing in a beauty pageant, and thus began her film career. After appearing in several American movies that were made overseas, Loren arrived in Hollywood in 1958.

With alluring performances in *Desire Under the Elms, Houseboat, The Black Orchard*, and *It Started in Naples*, Loren became synonymous with female sensual beauty throughout the 1960s and '70s. Especially popular were her roles opposite Italy's leading man, Marcello Mastroianni, including the movies *Yesterday, Today and Tomorrow* and *Marriage Italian-Style*; for the latter, she won a Best Actress Oscar nomination. Her acting career has continued in such films as *Grumpier Old Men* and *Messages*, and in TV roles. Loren eventually married Ponti, with whom she has two children, Carlo Jr. and Eduardo.

In *Sophia, Living and Loving*, written by A. E. Hotchner, the celebrated actress reminisced:

The first person I saw when I came to was Dr. de Watteville, who said, his face all smiles, "You have a fine baby boy." I embraced him, this man who had helped give me this most precious gift. Then there was Carlo embracing me and whispering joyful things in my ear.

The baby was in the incubator, but a few hours later, he was brought to me and placed in my arms. He had a little bandage on his bottom where de Watteville nicked him with the scalpel (he must have been as nervous as the rest of us). The baby had the beautiful round face of an apple, an apple insect with perfectly round blue eyes. What a strange moment that was, that first moment with the baby. A stranger put into my arms, feeling not at all that he had come from my body, a moment of bewilderment for me, until he turned his pink mouth to my nipple and put his tiny hands on my breast and sucked his first milk. Then we were joined as mother and child, and that special happiness, so long postponed, was mine forever.

Motherhood Is a Sacred Bond

Linda Hogan

Award-winning novelist, poet, and essayist Linda Hogan is descended from the Chickasaw Indians on her father's side and Europeans on her mother's. Published in 1993, her first novel, *Mean Spirit*, was nominated for a Pulitzer Prize. Hogan's subsequent diverse books include *Power: A Novel; The Book of Medicines: Poems; Intimate Nature: The Bond Between Women and Animals;* and *The Woman Who Watches Over the World: A Personal Memoir.* Hogan is a professor of English at the University of Colorado in Boulder. In the anthology *A Question of Balance*, she mused about motherhood:

> I still write daughter poems. I write about children and their relationship with their mother. I feel that the relationship between a mother and her child is one of the strongest and most holy bonds in existence, because in some way, part of the word

"mother" has to do with being the origin or the creator of something. I'm not sure the mother is the creator, but I think that mother and child have a creative bond and a creative energy that forms and shapes both of them.

Motherhood Makes You Grow

Helen Caldicott

Raised in Australia, Helen Caldicott trained as a physician and devoted herself to the treatment of children afflicted with cystic fibrosis. But it was in the political turmoil of the 1970s and '80s that she found her true calling. Resigning from Harvard Medical School's faculty, Helen helped found and was first president of Physicians for Social Responsibility (PSR) and the Women's Action for Nuclear Disarmament (WAND), two organizations at the forefront of the nuclear-freeze movement. Over the next decade, Caldicott brought her message to world leaders, to the media, and to audiences of thousands whom she roused with unique elegance. In 1985, PSR's umbrella affiliate, the International Physicians for the Prevention of Nuclear War, was the recipient of the Nobel Peace Prize.

Caldicott remains a tireless figure, advocating around the globe for peace and nuclear disarmament. In her autobiography, entitled *A Desperate Passion*, the influential physician recalled:

I went home from the hospital after ten days, and every morning when I picked Philip up from his bassinet, the sky was bluer and more luminous than it had been the day before. I was so full of love for him that I developed a stiff neck watching his face as he sucked milk from my breast, and the sound of warm milk gurgling down his hungry throat was the most fulfilling sound I had ever heard.

One day as we drove across a rickety temporary bridge spanning Canberra's new Lake Burley Griffin, I suddenly knew that I would willingly drown to save my baby. I had never felt like this about another human being before. In fact, I suddenly realized I was now an adult. No longer could I expect other people to make the world safe. I had to accept that the responsibility for the safety of this child, for his future—for that of all children in this nuclear age—was now mine. This was a profound turning point for me, a rite of passage from childhood to maturity.

Hillary Rodham Clinton

The former First Lady was dogged with controversy throughout Bill Clinton's tumultuous administration. In seeking to shape public policy on such issues as national health care, she often appeared argumentative and combative. But in her new position as U.S. senator from New York, Hillary Rodham Clinton has surprised even her most audible critics with a seemingly newfound genial and non-partisan problem-solving style. Virtually all observers of the American political scene expect her higher ambitions to manifest decisively ahead.

As cited in Claire Osborne's anthology, *The Unique Voice of Hillary Rodham Clinton*, the former First Lady remarked:

I think that we both learned from Chelsea. I remember one night when she was just a few weeks old, and I was rocking her because she was crying. I just looked at her and said, "Chelsea, you've never been a baby before, and I've never been a mother before, and we're just going to have to help each other get through this."

I think that our willingness to just learn from Chelsea, and respect who she is—the person she was meant to be—has helped us a lot.

Later, in a cover story for *Ladies Home Journal*, Hillary Rodham Clinton commented:

[The biggest challenge of motherhood is that] it's a delicate balance to the worrier, but also to recognize that you can't control everything. You can't even control everything in a ten-week-old's life, let alone a twenty-year-old's life. But I can't imagine not having been a mother—the things I learned about myself, and the kind of person I am. You see yourself reflected in your child as she grows through different stages. And you have to be constantly aware of what your strong feelings are without smothering this little person.

Jamie Lee Curtis

The daughter of film stars Tony Curtis and Janet Leigh, Jamie Lee Curtis has appeared in more than thirty-five films including *Drowning Mona, Virus, True Lies, A Fish Called Wanda, Trading Places*, and the popular *Halloween* "slashers." The adoption of daughter Annie inspired Curtis to write her best-known children's book, *Tell Me Again About the Night I Was Born*. Her other popular books include *Today I Feel Silly, When I was Little*, and *Where Do Balloons Go?*

In an interview for *Redbook*, Jamie Lee Curtis remarked:

What surprised me about myself [when I became a mother], truthfully, is that I'd get really angry at my daughter. As much as I wished for kids, raising them was hard. It's emotionally messy. All of a sudden, there's this personality, somebody with an opinion, who is saying no. I certainly had the capacity to love, but I was unaware that I could get angry. In life, all you can do is learn and get better. There are a lot of things I've had to let go of.

Rita Dove

Rita Dove became, at age forty, the youngest writer to be appointed Poet Laureate by the U.S. Library of Congress. Winner of a Pulitzer Prize for *Thomas and Beulah*, a 1986 collection of poems telling the two sides of her maternal grandparents' love story, Dove is a professor of creative writing at the University of Virginia in Charlottesville. Her literary work includes the novels *Through the Ivory Gate* and *Darker Face of the Earth*, and such poetry books as *On the Bus with Rosa Parks* and *Mother Love*. In the anthology *A Question of Balance*, Dove reflected on motherhood:

I could not have imagined, really, what it is like to be pregnant, to bear that responsibility. After she was born, for the first time in my life, I felt completely vulnerable to the world. I mean, we all feel vulnerable at certain times, but with a child there is this feeling that you would do anything to save her or protect her. And that makes you a hostage to reality, so to speak.

Sometimes the emotion is fear: "My God, I hope nothing happens to her." Sometimes, it's just an enormous feeling of vulnerability, having to be open. I don't think I could have imagined what that was like. I see it in my friends who don't have children or who have not been responsible for a child; they can be the most compassionate and caring people in the world, but they don't have that odd fragility that parents do.

Nicole Kidman

Though American-born, actress and producer Nicole Kidman grew up in Australia. She made her TV debut at the age of sixteen in *Bush Christmas*, which still airs in Australia each December. By the time Kidman made her first American film, *Dead Calm*, she was already famous in Australia. After appearing opposite Tom Cruise in *Days of Thunder*, they married on Christmas Day, 1990, after a whirlwind romance.

Subsequently struggling to break free from her media identity as "Tom Cruise's wife," Kidman appeared in such high-profile movies as *Batman Returns, The Peacemaker*, and *Practical Magic*. Soon after the couple's racy film together, *Eyes Wide Shut*, was released, they announced their marital separation. Since then, Kidman's stellar performances in *Moulin Rouge, The Others*, and *The Hours* have earned both critical and popular acclaim.

As the parent with Cruise of two adopted children, Kidman commented in a *Good Housekeeping* interview:

Oh, yes, from the point [of having a child] on, your life really is so much about somebody else. There are other people you're responsible for. And no matter what happens in your life, you have to pick yourself up every day, because they look toward you. You're their role model. And when they're twenty-two years old, you're the person they'll say they admire. That's really what I hope for: that someday my kids will say, "I admire my mother."

I beat myself up so much as a mother, over everything I think I'm doing wrong. But as my mom says, "Motherhood is riddled with guilt." And you've go to go easy on yourself, I guess. This year, I've only worked four weeks, and I'm not working for the rest of the year.

It's been an important time for my kids to have their mom in the house . . . in the kitchen in the morning, making breakfast. My daughter said to me last night, "I just love hearing your voice calling up saying, Bella! Connor! Here's breakfast!" I used to love that—because my mother used to do the same thing. It's so strange how you pass on the same routines, how the littlest thing becomes something you remember.

Reese Witherspoon

Petite former Nashville debutante Reese Witherspoon left Stanford University at the age of twenty to pursue a full-time acting career. Quickly moving from quirky, attention-getting parts in *Pleasantville* and *Election*, she entered the ranks of stardom with her performances

171

in *Cruel Intentions, Legally Blonde*, and more recently, *Sweet Home Alabama*.

In Style magazine featured Witherspoon's reflections on becoming a mother at the age of twenty-three:

"We love being parents. We love the simple joy of watching Ava in the morning. It's really soothing. What we do is so hectic and exhausting, it's so nice to have that comfort and stability at home."

The transition into motherhood, however, wasn't entirely easy for Witherspoon. "I was really nervous," she says, "I had never held a baby until I held my own. But the hardest part for me was not sleeping. I did not sleep for six months. It was awful."

As Ava has gotten older, the challenge for Witherspoon has changed from getting her daughter to sleep to passing on the old-fashioned values she holds dear. "You hear that the kid next door has a fire truck and you're like, 'A real fire truck?' 'Yeah, a real one.' It's all about what you instill in your children. You just have to fight a little more."

She adds:

"I was surprised when the ultrasound revealed that I was having a girl. I was convinced I was having a boy. And I was completely confounded by the fact that I wasn't in control of the situation; that I was being introduced to a different individual coming into my life."

Nurturing a Baby with Disabilities

Laura San Giacomo

Laura San Giacomo grew up in suburban New Jersey and completed a fine arts degree at Carnegie Mellon University with an emphasis on acting. After early television appearances in the series *Crime Story* and *The Equalizer*, Laura San Giacomo became a 1999 Golden Globe nominee as Best Actress in a Series, Comedy or Musical for *Just Shoot Me*. She made an impressive film debut in the 1989 breakthrough independent film *Sex, Lies, and Videotape*, which won the Palme D'Or grand prize at the Cannes Film Festival and earned the actress the prestigious New Generation Award from the Los Angeles Film Critics Association. Her subsequent film roles have included *Pretty Woman, Under Suspicion, Stuart Saves His Family*, and *The Apocalypse*.

In 1997, San Giacomo made her TV sitcom debut in *Just Shoot Me*, co-starring George Segal and David Spade. Her main reason to take the role was the birth of her first child, Mason. In a cover story interview for *Rosie*, San Giacomo commented:

On the positive side [of being a mother], I never knew that I had so much energy. Even after a long day on the set, there's a reserve I manage to tap into because I love him so much.

The most difficult part has been learning to set boundaries: since I'd rather not see him scream and cry, it's tempting to be too permissive. I like to be my son's friend, but sometimes I have to be his parent, especially since his dad isn't around all the time. . . .

When Mason came out, he was having seizures and was blue. After I started to come to, they told me he was in the Intensive Care Unit on a respirator and they were trying to drain his lungs. He had aspirated the meconium while he was trying to breathe. So they were draining his lungs, and he had tubes hooked up to every part of his body. They told me he was having seizures, and they were trying to stop the seizures.

At two and a half days [after birth], they discovered that he had had a stroke. We know that there has been a brain injury. We know that is where the seizure comes from, but I still don't get what's going on. So after four days I left the hospital, and he was still in the Intensive Care Unit.

But I got to hold him, and that was my Thanksgiving Day present. I felt like there was a spotlight from heaven shining down on me. I felt like my life was important, and that in this moment, I was very special. And that is what it is all about. This is it.

Kelly Preston

Born in Honolulu, model and actress Kelly Preston has enjoyed considerable success from an early age. While still attending high school, she was discovered by a fashion photographer who helped her get gigs in TV commercials and an audition for *The Blue Lagoon*. Though Preston lost out on that role to Brooke Shields, she gained attention for her comedic roles in *Mischief* and *Secret Admirer*, which were both released in 1985, when she was twenty-three. After a short marriage, Preston had live-in romances with George Clooney and Charlie Sheen, before meeting John Travolta when they were filming *The Experts* in Toronto. The two met again while filming separately in Vancouver and were married in 1991. Preston's career blossomed after *Jerry Maguire*, and her subsequent movies include *For Love of the Game, Addicted to Love, Nothing to Lose*, and *Battlefield Earth*.

Good Housekeeping recently featured the actress in an interview:

Kelly Preston's smile disappears. Her face clouds over. She looks as if she may start crying.

"I was a basket case. I was on the floor, my knees gave way, I was sobbing. Just sobbing, sobbing, sobbing. Because I was maybe going to lose my baby."

Her then two-year-old son, Jett, was in the next room in the hospital, hooked up to an IV and monitors. The doctors had just told her that Jett was probably suffering from Kawasaki syndrome, a rare childhood disease that causes inflammation of the blood vessels. If left untreated, it can damage the coronary arteries, and it is also a leading cause of heart disease among children.

"I was afraid he would die," her husband, John Travolta adds, "I've never been that upset in my life. I had a lot of grief to deal with, because Jetty was the best thing that ever happened to me, and I just couldn't bear to watch him suffer."

"It was so scary," says Kelly, thirty-nine. "I'd never even heard of the disease." But after Jett's recovery, she and John concluded that the potentially fatal disease, the causes of which are unknown, was brought on by toxic chemicals in the environment. . . . This marked the beginning of Kelly's environmental activism and her commitment to helping other parents protect their children from this insidious danger. . . . Now she's an outspoken, hardworking board member of the Children's Health Environmental Coalition.

Nurturing a Sick Baby

Grandma Moses (Anna Mary Robertson)

"If I didn't start painting, I would have raised chickens," quipped Anna Mary Robertson, a crusty, feisty, upstate New York farm woman and grandmother who gained fame in the mid-twentieth century for her primitive artistry. After raising ten children and working hard at a variety of jobs, Anna devoted herself full-time to art in the 1930s, when she began exhibiting her work—mostly of placid rural life—in county fairs. "Discovered" in the window of a Hoosick Falls, New York, drugstore by a Manhattan art collector in 1938, Anna's paintings were soon placed on exhibit in the Museum of Modern Art and eventually featured in leading art galleries and publications. Anna became a celebrity over the next two decades, and her one hundredth birthday in 1960 was virtually a day of national celebration. Anna died the following year. On her headstone, the inscription reads: "Her primitive paintings captured the spirit and preserved the scene of a vanishing countryside."

In *Grandma Moses, My Life's Story*, edited by Otto Kalir, the famous artist recalled:

Brother Fred was a baby then, about three months old, and he was hungry, and cried and kept crying. We couldn't stop him. Mother was quite sick with the measles. Father said, "He's hungry," so I went to the pantry and fixed him a coffee cup full of bread and milk, and I used a good deal of the top milk, with sugar on it. I set it on the edge of the stove to keep it warm, then took Fred and wrapped a cloth under his chin and commenced feeding him that bread and milk. I fed all of it to him. He went off to sleep. He had never had anything but breast milk up to that time.

Fred slept all night and way into the next morning. When father came in about 11 o'clock, I asked him to look at the baby, which he did, and he said, "Fred is all right." He was still asleep at 3 o'clock in the afternoon, when mother said, "I wish you would bring me the baby, he hadn't ought to sleep like this."

I went to the cradle and picked Fred up, but I didn't dare uncover his face . . . for I feared I should not have fed him bread and milk and that he was dead. As mother lifted the veil from his face, she said, "Oh my goodness!" and then I knew he was gone! I turned to look, and his face was as red as red could be. He was all broken out in measles!

But Fred has lived to be an old man, and is in his seventies now.

Opening to Parenthood

Menachem Schneerson

Rabbi Menachem Schneerson was the dynamic leader of the Lubavitcher Hasidic movement for more than forty years. Born and raised in Russia, he immigrated to Brooklyn, New York, on the eve of World War II and helped to create a worldwide network of religious schools, institutions, and agencies rooted in traditional Jewish precepts. The recipient of many governmental awards around the globe for his educational efforts, Rabbi Schneerson emphasized the importance of parenting as a spiritual activity. In *Toward a Meaningful Life*, he wisely advised:

> Childhood is not just for the child. It allows parents to tap the purest part of themselves: their souls. Especially in our turbulent generation, it is often the children who end up teaching the most profound values to their parents.
>
> So when you spend time with your child—or any child—do not be casual about the experience. Look at the child intently and

realize: God has given you this gift to nurture and care for, to teach good habits and the difference between right and wrong. Your attitude toward this child and the sensibilities you impart will be crucial to how [its] life develops and influences others. Now, how much time can you possibly devote to this enormous responsibility? And most important of all: Allow your child to be himself and to teach you how to live a more meaningful life.

Planning for the Birth

Lucille Ball

Lucille Ball was among America's most popular actresses for more than fifty years. Her career began in stage dancing; she then moved on to film. Using her comedic talent in her series *I Love Lucy, The Lucy Show*, and *Here's Lucy*, she shattered many stereotypes about femininity and "ladylike behavior." Countless episodes showed her scheming to outwit her controlling husband, Ricky, and achieve her goals. It's no accident that Lucille Ball became the first woman in America to own a major entertainment studio, Desilu Productions. Yet playfulness was always vital to her character and dated back to her childhood experiences.

In her memoir *Love, Lucy*, the celebrated actress recalled:

Desi and I were so excited and happy, planning our first big venture together. I thought that *I Love Lucy* was a pleasant little situation comedy that might even survive its first season. But my main thoughts centered on the baby. The nursery wing was now complete and I planned to have a natural delivery late in June. And so I happily waited, and waited, thirty pounds heavier than ever before. I was so proud of that big stomach of mine. Desi, knowing that my grandmother Flora Belle had been one of five sets of twins, expected triplets.

The weeks passed and still no baby. Finally, my obstetrician decided on a caesarian delivery. Lucie Desirée Arnaz was lying sideways with her hand just under my rib cage; when they performed the caesarian, the surgical knife missed her face by a hairsbreadth. But it did miss her; she was complete, healthy, and beautiful.

Lyricist Eddie Maxwell wrote the words to a song in her honor, "There's a Brand-New Baby at Our House" and Desi sat up all night with his guitar composing the music. The next day, the proud papa passed out Havana cigars to his entire studio audience and introduced his new daughter and that song to the world on his new CBS radio show, *Tropical Trip*. Later on, it was used on the show when Lucy Ricardo had the baby.

Lucie's coming changed our life completely. Before, there had been two professional people in the house, discussing deals and money matters and scripts. Now suddenly there was a fragile little new spark of life there, affecting everything we thought or did.

Praying to Have a Child

Hannah of the Bible

For thousands of years, infertility has been a cause of mental anguish for many women. In virtually all the world's major religions, the birth of a child is a cause for thanksgiving and gratitude to the Supreme Being for bringing this blessing into our lives. In the Hebrew Bible, the story of Hannah (presented in the *Book of Samuel*) beautifully reminds us that childbirth is indeed a miracle:

> Because the Lord had closed her womb . . . Hannah wept and would not eat. And Elkanah, her husband, said to her, "Hannah, why do you weep? And why do you not eat? And why is your heart sad? Am I not more to you than ten sons?"
>
> After they had eaten and drunk in Shiloh, Hannah rose. Now Eli the priest was sitting on the seat beside the doorpost of the temple of the Lord. She was deeply distressed and prayed to the Lord, and wept bitterly. . . . As she continued praying before

the Lord, Eli observed her mouth. Hannah was speaking in her heart; only her lips moved, and her voice was not heard; therefore Eli took her to be a drunken maiden. And Eli said to her, "How long will you be drunken? Put away your wine from you."

But Hannah answered. "No, my lord, I am a woman severely troubled; I have drunk neither wine nor strong drink, but I have been pouring out my soul before the Lord. Do not regard your maidservant as a base woman, for all along I have been speaking out of my great anxiety and vexation."

Then Eli answered, "Go in peace, and the God of Israel grant your petition which you have made to him." And she said, "Let your maidservant find favor in your eyes." Then the woman went her way and ate, and her countenance was no longer sad.

They rose early in the morning and worshipped before the Lord; then they went back to their house at Ramah. And Elkanah knew Hannah his wife, and the Lord remembered her; and in due time Hannah conceived and bore a son, and she called his name Samuel, for she said, "I have asked him of the Lord."

LaVera Draisin

LaVera Draisin is a board-certified physician in the San Francisco Bay area who specialized in family medicine from a cross-cultural viewpoint. Former director of the Health Studies Program of the California Institute for Integral Studies, Draisin practiced medicine on a Navajo reservation for several years. Not long after this work, she authored the well-received essay, "Birth, Creation Stories, and the Spiritual Journey," which originally appeared in my anthology *Opening the Inner Gates:*

I entered the doorway and saw my husband seated at the westernmost wall of the one-room dwelling. I was led to the center of the room, where I sat on a beautiful woven blanket placed on the dry earthen floor. The medicine man sat to the left of the doorway, arranging his medicine bundle.

Opening his corn pollen pouch, he removed some of the coarse white powder and anointed the support beam at the east end of the hogan, followed by the south beam, the west, and lastly the north supports. Moving sunwise, he prepared the stage, as I was told, for a reenactment of the first creation. Continuing to sprinkle pollen within the hogan, he knelt down beside me.

Again removing corn pollen from his pouch, he annointed my feet and legs and continued all the way to the top of my head. After making a final offering to the earth and the sky, he sat himself away from me and began a long droning chant. In the precise manner passed on generation after generation before him, he sang a passage from the Navajo creation story to bring forth the blessings. . . .

185

Although I did not speak the language and could not follow the story held in the songs, prayers, and chants that he uttered, I was fully aware of the power held in that room, and in that moment I silently recited prayers of my own, experiencing gratitude and asking to be open to all blessings. . . . I focused my attention on the sounds and pulsating rhythms of his voice, allowing myself to drift into a deep meditative state beyond sounds, beyond thought, and beyond time and space.

At some point, I physically felt that I had grown larger than the hogan, as if my consciousness had filled the entire universe. The medicine man, my husband, my Navajo friend Ada, even the landscape were no longer separate from me. Somehow we seemed joined as one unity. . . .

Every stage of pregnancy reflects changes of the creation story. When a Navajo mother in labor prepares to bring forth her child, she becomes both the embodiment of creation itself and Changing Woman, the Earth Mother. When the emerging newborn is pushed out into this world through the mother holding on to a colorful hanging sash belt, it is one of the Hero Twins returning to a Rainbow Bridge again and again as time continues, ready to restore peace and security on his people. This is the mirroring of two realms—the participation mystique—where the creation of the present and the first creation of eternity come together in an omnipresent and never-ending cycle of completion. . . .

Every birth is unique, as are all individual stories, yet each birth and each story are part of the one story of creation. . . . Illuminated by a consciousness of beauty, my experience created a personal new story to mirror the larger story of Creation.

Preparing a Toddler's Birthday Party

Camryn Manheim

Award-winning TV actress and best-selling author *(Wake Up, I'm Fat!)* Camryn Manheim grew up in Peoria, Illinois. Her mother was a teacher and her father a math professor. After earning a master's degree in fine arts from New York University, she worked as a sign language interpreter and then became involved in theater work. Manheim established her film career in the '90s with roles in *The Road to Wellville, Deadly Whispers, Romy and Michelle's High School Reunion*, and *What Planet Are You From?* She is best known for starring in the TV hit *The Practice*.

People weekly recently featured the actress and her toddler:

Manheim recently learned that nothing, not even a birthday bash for a one-year-old, can be done on a small scale in Los Angeles.

"I really wanted a small party," says Manheim, forty-one, who is celebrating her son Milo's first birthday this month. "But this is the funny thing about small birthday parties—I invited twelve children, but I forgot that about half of the kids have brothers and sisters that you have to invite. So twelve turned into twenty, which turned into forty adults. It's ridiculous."

The single actress, who also stars in HBO's *The Laramie Project*, did ponder an alternative course of action, albeit briefly. "I wouldn't have a party if I could put a hat on Milo and take a good picture," says Manheim with a laugh. "But you can't do that. Having bubbles just doesn't thrill him anymore. I've actually got to entertain him. So I'm having a dozen itty-bitty puppies brought over to run around and play with the kids. It's all about the photo opportunities."

Raising a Community Baby

Andrew Young

Andrew Young's career as a civil rights activist and public official has spanned more than forty years. Raised in New Orleans, he became a minister, and in 1960 joined the Southern Christian Leadership Conference spearheaded by Dr. Martin Luther King Jr. The two worked together closely, and as the group's executive director (1964–1970), Young took an active role in ending segregation throughout the South. Shortly thereafter, he became the first African American to represent Georgia in Congress since 1871, and he served under President Jimmy Carter as U.S. representative to the United Nations. Holding office as mayor of Atlanta for eight years, Young remains a national figure in the African-American community.

In his semi-autobiography, entitled *An Easy Burden: The Civil Rights Movement and the Transformation of America*, Young reminisced:

I did finally come to accept the fact that folk in the rural black South were quite formal. In Thomasville, I was called "Reb" or "Rev" or "Rev. Young." No one called me "Andrew," which would have been fine, or "son," which I would have hated. I made it a practice to address adults as Mr. or Mrs. because local whites called them by their first names, which they deeply resented. I only called people by their first names if I was on very intimate terms with them; and if they were my elders, never. It was insulting to hear whites calling an elderly black woman "Betty" or "Daisy" or "Rometta" when they were hardly acquaintances, much less friends. Jean was called by her first name fairly often, but mostly she was "Mrs. Young," even though she was considerably younger than most of the women in our churches. . . .

Our oldest daughter, Andrea, was born our first year in Thomasville. While Jean was at school, Mrs. Laura Hayes, a wonderful friend, helped baby-sit. During services, Jean scarcely had a chance to hold the baby because the women passed her around the congregation. People in Thomasville had that small-town openness and friendliness; because so many helped take care of Andrea she was raised as the "community baby."

Recalling a Pensive Baby

Mark Twain

Mark Twain, the pen name of Missouri-born Samuel Clemens, is one of America's most intriguing literary figures. In such late-nineteenth-century novels as *The Adventures of Huckleberry Finn, The Prince and the Pauper*, and *A Connecticut Yankee in King Arthur's Court*, Twain combined homespun humor with biting social criticism. But as a father and husband, he was tender hearted.

In his *Autobiography*, Twain mused:

Susy was born the 19th of March, 1872. The summer seasons of her childhood were spent at Quarry Farm on the hills east of Elmira, New York; the other seasons of the year at the home in Hartford. We removed to Hartford in 1871 and presently built a house. Like other children, she was blithe and happy, fond of play; *unlike* the average of children, she was at times much given to retiring within herself and trying to search out the hidden meanings of the deep things that make the puzzle and pathos of human existence, and in all the ages, have baffled the inquirer and mocked him.

"Mama, what is it all for?" asked Susy, preliminarily stating the above details in her own halting language, after long brooding in the privacy of the nursery.

Recalling A Sister's Birth

Myra Gardner Pierce

Actress Ava Gardner (the younger sister of Myra Gardner Pierce) is best remembered for her roles in now-classic movies like *Showboat, The Bible*, and *The Night of the Iguana*. Her other celebrated films include *The Snows of Kilimanjaro, The Barefoot Contessa*, and an Oscar-nominated performance opposite her screen idol, Clark Gable, in *Mogambo*.

Born on Christmas Eve, 1922, in rural North Carolina, Ava was the youngest of seven children. When she was two, her parents opened a boarding house for teachers at the rural Brogden School, and several years later, they operated another teacher's boarding house in the Rock Ridge community near Wilson township. Ava grew up as a pretty, risk-taking tomboy who was happiest running barefoot through the fields. During a visit to her older sister Beatrice and her photograper-husband Larry Tarr in New York City, Ava posed for photos. Larry displayed one in his studio window; it led to an MGM screen test and a movie contract in 1941. Beatrice went on to Hollywood with Ava and assisted in her skyrocketing career, with immensely publicized marriages to Mickey Rooney, bandleader Artie Shaw, and then Frank Sinatra along the way. At the age of thirty-three, Gardner moved to Madrid, Spain, and then settled in London for most of her subsequent life—returning often to America for her film career and to visit relatives in rural North Carolina. Ava remained friendly with her ex-husbands and enjoyed a complex relationship with tycoon Howard Hughes. Though never having children, she doted on her nieces and nephews.

In *Ava, My Story*, the birth of the renowned actress was recalled by her older sister Myra:

I was seven years old when Ava was born, and I remember it very well. It was Christmas Eve, and my brother Jack and I were sent away from home for a little while. I still believed in Santa Claus back then, and I was worried, afraid he wouldn't come if we weren't there. I guess that was kind of silly, but at the moment Santa Claus meant more to me. I probably didn't realize what was going to happen. . . .

Because there were seven years between Ava and me, I guess a baby was not expected when she came along. Because of that, she was sort of special, and everybody did dote on her. She had naturally curly hair that Mama had to brush every morning before she'd go to school, and Ava always hated that. But in the first year of her life, we thought she was never going to have any hair at all. She was kind of a baldheaded baby; she didn't grow a lot until she was about a year old.

Recalling a Stressful Birth

Melanie Griffith and Antonio Banderas

Raised in New York City, actess Melanie Griffith is best known for starring in such films as *Crazy in Alabama*, *Mulholland Falls*, and *Working Girl*. In 1995, she met the Spanish actor Antonio Banderas—who had previously appeared in such films as *Miami Rhapsody* and *Desperado*—while on the set of the film *Two Much*, and they married in London the following year.

In an interview for *In Style* magazine, the two jovially reminisced about their daughter's birth.

"The day Stella was born, I had to climb over the wall out there because we couldn't get out the front gate," says Griffith, laughing as she recalls how she and Banderas sneaked past a horde of paparazzi so she could get to a nearby hospital.

"We had a rental car waiting, and we covered ourselves with a blanket in the backseat," says Banderas, also laughing. A second later, however, all his mirth evaporates, and he goes as still as a matador between passes. "That night was the happiest night of my life. At 9:18 Stella was born. She had problems at first—nothing important in the end, but three rounds of the umbilical cord were wrapped around her neck. I thought she was dead. It took a minute for her to react. And that minute was the longest minute of my life."

Banderas then began to laugh, but was also fighting back tears. "Oh, my God, it was such a moment!"

Receiving News of Fatherhood

Colin Powell

Raised in the Bronx by immigrant parents from Jamaica, Colin Powell rose steadily through the ranks and became one of America's most prominent military figures during the Gulf War. He has subsequently served as secretary of state under President George W. Bush. Though advocating an internationalist perspective, Powell has also addressed the importance of knowing one's roots. In his autobiography *My American Journey*, Powell recollected:

> The day after the mortar attack a resupply helicopter hovered into view over the camp. In the mail was a letter from my mother. I planted myself under a tree and read the usual family chitchat. "Oh, by the way," Mom had written, "we are absolutely delighted about the baby."

What baby? What had happened to the baby letter? Was Alma all right? Was it a boy or girl? I had the radio operator raise the base camp on the ancient AN/GRC-9, and we managed to get patched through to Quang Tri. The letter had suffered from something not unheard of in military operations, a failure of communication. The envelope, clearly marked, was sitting in a stack of undelivered mail.

"Tell them I want it read *now*," I told the radio operator, and that was how I learned of the early arrival of Michael Kevin Powell, born March 23, 1963, in the Holy Family Catholic Hospital in Birmingham. He was reverse-named after Kevin Michael Schwar, one of the sons of our Fort Bragg samaritans, Joe and Pat Schwar.

My emotions at this time were an odd mixture—elation that I had a healthy son and a strong wife: bewilderment as I looked around the alien world that had happened to me; and a nagging anxiety I had come close to being killed, never knowing I had become a father. A family back home was depending on me, including a small new person. I wanted desperately to see this child. I had to make it through the year.

Rejoicing After the Birth

Elie Wiesel

Elie Wiesel is probably the world's most respected and influential Holocaust survivor and spokesperson. Born into a religious Jewish-Romanian family in the village of Sighet, Wiesel was sixteen years old when he was deported, along with his entire family and all his Jewish neighbors, to the Auschwitz death camp. His parents and younger sister, Tsipouka, were killed, but young Wiesel was forced into slave labor at Buchenwald, another German death camp. Following the end of World War II, Wiesel settled in France, where he studied at the Sorbonne and became a journalist. In 1956, he relocated to the United States and acquired citizenship.

Wiesel's first book, *Night*, chronicled his experiences at the hands of the Nazis, and was followed by works including *Dawn, The Town Beyond the Wall, A Beggar in Jerusalem*, and many others. In 1985, Wiesel was awarded the U.S. Congressional Gold Medal of Achievement, and the following year, he won the Nobel Peace Prize. Traveling frequently around the globe as a lecturer, Wiesel holds a professorship at Boston University.

In his memoir *And the Sea Is Never Full*, Wiesel recounted:

The Hasidim are shouting. Open yourselves to joy. Easily said. For my generation, no joy can be whole. I look at my son who will never know his paternal grandparents. Silently I beg them to protect the one who has been called upon to assure their continuity. Protect him, beloved ancestors. Thanks to him, the line will not become extinct. It is a line that goes back far, all the way to the Sh'la. And to the Tossafot Yom Tov. And to Rashi, thus to King David.

Protect your descendant. . . . Guide him to the right path. And may he make you proud of what his soul becomes. Mother, protect your grandson. I don't know where you are resting, but please lean over his crib and help me sing him lullabies. Tell him your wondrous and strange tales that made me sleep peacefully. And you, father, protect his dreams. Help him live his child's life. Help me.

"May this little one grow up and enter the world of study, marriage, and good deeds." It is Heschel who recites this customary prayer.

Beloved ancestors, please say: Amen.

Reminiscing About Childhood

Bruce Willis

For more than a dozen years, Bruce Willis has ranked among Hollywood's most popular actors, starring in such films as *The Fifth Element, Unbreakable*, and *The Sixth Sense*. Raised in blue-collar New Jersey, he left college to pursue an acting career. After appearing for several years opposite Cybill Shepherd in the hit TV show *Moonlighting*, Willis reached stardom status with the 1988 movie *Die Hard*, in which he played a New York City policeman, and which spawned two sequels. He and his ex-wife Demi Moore have three daughters.

In an *Esquire* interview, Willis confided:

When I was kid, I stuttered. Really bad—I could hardly get a sentence out. When you're a stutterer, there's always this nagging feeling in the back of your head, scratching on a nerve. You're making people uncomfortable because they want to help you so they try to finish your sentence, and it makes you stutter even more, because now you're locked into this cycle. My parents helped me by just treating me normally. Compassion and love are great tools under those circumstances.

When you're confronted with adversity, you have two choices: Succumb to it, or walk through the fire. I thought: "Yes, I do stutter. But if I can make you laugh, maybe I can take your mind off it." Like a magic trick. So I always tried to crack my friends up, doing things that were funny to people at that age at that time, though they certainly weren't very funny to my teachers.

I didn't want my stutter to hold me back, so I took part in a school play. I must have been in the eighth grade. I went onstage, and it was miraculous! Then, when I came off the stage, it came back. Any role that took me out of who I really was took away the stutter. It made me want to act more and more. I white-knuckled the stuttering for years, and eventually beat it. By the time I got to college, I knew I wanted to be an actor. . . .

When I was a kid, forty-five seemed old, really old. I don't feel the years on my shoulders, but I see the lines in my face. That's what laughing for a long time will do. In my heart, I'm still twenty-five, but I know I'm forty-five. I've stopped drinking. Having kids is a good reason not to be drunk. I want to stick around for my kids. I want to be able to run around with their kids.

Respecting Children's Imagination

Steven Spielberg

Steven Spielberg is undoubtedly the most popular filmmaker in the world today. He grew up in a middle-class Jewish family in Cincinnati during the 1950s and received encouragement from his doting mother to pursue imaginative and creative activities. Since the age of twenty-eight, with his blockbuster *Jaws*, Spielberg has directed a series of hugely profitable and aesthetically acclaimed movies including *Close Encounters of the Third Kind, E.T., Raiders of the Lost Ark, The Color Purple, Jurassic Park, Schindler's List*, and *Minority Report*. At a UCLA graduation ceremony, Spielberg, who has a large family, reflected:

> My films have been often accused of—or, as I like to think, applauded for—having childlike qualities. I do believe that the greatest quality that we can possess is curiosity, a genuine interest in the world around us. The most used word—and I have

five kids, so I know what I'm talking about—the most used word in a child's vocabulary is "Why?" From this simple question and such basic curiosity, great acts are born. . . .

The child's brave spirit is the angel inside each of us, the force that often seems to shrink as we grow bigger. Still, it's there, and we have a responsibility to keep it strong, just as we work our bodies to keep the muscles from atrophying. It doesn't matter what path we take; we have to remain curious and fearless.

Respecting Your Child's Growth

Betty Ford

Betty Ford (née Bloomer) was a professional model and dancer in New York City before returning to her hometown of Grand Rapids, Michigan. After her first, brief marriage ended, she met Gerald Ford through a mutual friend, and the two were wedded in 1948. Throughout his thirty-year political career, culminating in his appointment to the U.S. presidency by Richard Nixon in conjunction with his resignation in 1974, Betty was a loyal wife and mother of four. Soon after leaving the White House, she gained wide attention by publicly admitting her chemical dependency problem and seeking therapeutic help. Today she remains active as a fund-raiser and spokesperson for the Betty Ford Center and an advocate for those with similar difficulties.

As cited by Bill Adler in his anthology, *Motherhood: A Celebration*, the former First Lady pithily observed:

I feel that God gives us these children and expects us to do the best we can with them for a certain time. Then they are on their own.

Liv Ullmann

Though born a citizen of Norway, Liv Ullmann did not set foot in her homeland until she was seven years old. Deciding on an acting career, she studied in London in the late 1950s. After appearing in Norwegian stage productions, Ullmann made her film debut with *Persona*, directed by Ingmar Bergman. The two became close professionally and romantically, and had a child, Linn, together. During the 1970s, Ullmann was honored with numerous New York City Film Critic Awards for her roles in such movies as *Cries and Whispers, Scenes from a Marriage*, and *Face to Face*. Though no longer appearing in films, she has emerged as a theatrical and TV director.

In her memoir, *Choices*, Ullman wrote these words to young Linn:

Child, do not look upon me with such eyes. I see in them that you are angry. That even if, just a short while ago, we were laughing together, I must have done something to displease you.

If only you knew that reaching forty is as hard as being your age. I know as little about all the different emotions that are invading me as you understand the changing within your body. Both of us will have to wait a few months or a few years to find out who we are going to be next. But it's all going to happen.

Your thin little body will bloom, and your wonderful black eyelashes will cast shadows on pink cheeks when you blush with your secrets; and my body will never again be as graceful and my movements as powerful and effortless as when I was innocent about them. Maybe I will even look at you and envy you and then be miserable with shame. I watch you now, leaning against a tree under the shimmer of white blossoms. You know nothing of the adventure that is ahead of you as you become a woman. Today you only suffer, unaware that all the time you are opening up like a rose.

Seeing a Stressful Birth

Lance Armstrong

National and world champion cyclist, two-time Olympian, renowned humanitarian role model, cancer survivor, and three-time winner of the Tour de France, Lance Armstrong is among the most celebrated and charismatic figures in the cycling world. Raised in Plano, Texas, he showed tremendous athletic prowess by the age of thirteen, and five years later he qualified for the 1989 junior world championship in Moscow. Diagnosed with metastatic testicular cancer in 1996, he formed the Lance Armstrong Foundation within months of his diagnosis and stunned even loyalist fans when he began racing—and winning tournaments—soon after completing effective medical treatment.

In his memoir *It's Not About the Bike*, Armstrong reported on his son's birth:

> When they pulled him out, he was tiny, and blue, and covered with birth fluids. They placed him on Kik's chest, and we hud-

dled together. But he wasn't crying. He just made a couple of small, mewlike sounds. The delivery-room staff seemed concerned that he wasn't making more noise. *Cry*, I thought. Another moment passed, and Luke still didn't cry. ***Come on, cry.*** I could feel the room grow tense around me.

"He's going to need a little help," someone said. . . .

[Soon] they had him on oxygen, with a tiny mask over his face.

Cry, please. Please, please cry.

I was petrified. At that moment, I would have done anything just to hear him scream, absolutely anything. Whatever I knew about fear was completely eclipsed in that delivery room. I was scared when I was diagnosed with cancer, and I was scared when I was being treated, but it was nothing compared to what I felt when they took our baby away from us. I felt totally helpless, because this time it wasn't me who was sick, it was somebody else. It was my son.

They removed the mask. He opened his mouth, and scrunched his face, and all of a sudden he let out a big, strong "Whaaaaaaaaa!!" He screamed like a world-class, champion screamer. With that, his color changed, and everyone seemed to relax. They brought him back to us. I held him, and I kissed him.

Seeing Babies Mystically

Bronson Alcott

The New England philosopher-educator Bronson Alcott eagerly kept a journal to record his children's development. More broadly, Alcott hoped to use these impressions to create a new vision of human nature and its divine connection. In February 1833, he wrote in a journal entry:

> The observation and record of results in the experience of my two children, though extremely crude and unsatisfactory, occupied a place in my attention. . . . The leading idea which [is] this:
>
> The human soul has had a primordial experience in the infinite Spirit. The infinite is embodied in the finite, to be developed and returned again to the source of infinite energy from whence it sprang. This is [a] spiritual and earthly experience, and all the phenomena of humanity arise from the union and evolution of these elements. The finite is but the return of the soul on the path of the infinite—the wheeling orb attracted toward, and yet preserved in the cycle of, the central sphere.

Seeing Children's Joy

William Blake

Visionary poet, artist, and engraver William Blake had little influence on his British contemporaries in the late eighteenth century. But in the decades after his death, he steadily gained a stature that remains towering today. Though Blake and his beloved wife were childless, he wrote brilliant verse celebrating the presence of babies in the world. Blake's first book, *Songs of Innocence*, contained these poems:

INFANT JOY

"I have no name;
I am but two days old."
What shall I call thee?
"I happy am,
Joy is my name."
Sweet joy befall thee!

Pretty joy!
Sweet joy but two days old,
Sweet joy I call thee;
Thou dost smile.
I sing the while,
Sweet joy befall thee.

NURSE'S SONG

When the voices of children are heard on the green
And laughing is heard on the hill,
My heart is a rest within my breast
And every thing is still.

"Then come home, my children, the sun is gone down
And the dews of night arise;
Come, come, leave off play, and let us away
Till the morning appears in the skies."

"No, no, let us play, for it is yet day
And we cannot go to sleep;
Besides, in the sky the little birds fly
And the hills are cover'd with sheep."

"Well, well, go & play till the light fades away
And then go home to bed."
The little ones leaped & shouted & laughed
And all the hills echoed.

Sharing News About Your Baby

Lidian Emerson

Lidian Jackson Emerson, the second wife of Ralph Waldo Emerson, America's leading nineteenth-century philosopher, was well known for her wit and verbal eloquence. Born in Plymouth, Massachussetts, she and her two siblings were raised by relatives after their mother died early from tuberculosis. With a highly disciplined mind, Lidian was admirably self-taught, and, together with eight women friends in Plymouth, she organized a Reading Society and issued a newsletter called *The Wisdom of the Nine*.

She and Ralph Waldo Emerson married in 1835, four years after his first wife's death, and the year before his first book, *Nature*, was published to wide acclaim. From the outset, their mutual attraction was intense. Lidian shared her husband's mystical, poetic outlook on life, and she became close with several of his friends including Henry David Thoreau. She was a devoted mother, and as her four children entered their teenage years, Lidian's advice was always *common sense:* "Our confidence in you is entire, and there is no need to give you minute directions."

In December 1841, Lidian penned these happy words to her sister:

I can still tell you that we are going on prosperously, being myself able to go about the house and the baby growing finely. We thought she a plump little damsel when she first appeared, but now she quite excels her former self in that respect. Her limbs are though pretty at first much improved in form, remarkably taper and firm for such a young thing. She is still the most comfortable and contended of babies—never has cried in the night, and never been "worrysome" by day, except one fair noon. I have not had one "ill time."

All that has not been right with is that I have not been able to make up my sleep in the day what the baby deprives me of by night. She comes to me twice in the night, as I cannot make her take enough before my bedtime to last her till morning, she is sleepy.

Her being born three weeks too soon, has interfered with my wish to give her regular habits. She is not awake more than three hours a day, but then is very bright.

Showing Sensitivity to Your Child

J.K. Rowling

Born in Gloucestershire, England, the world's most popular children's author is the daughter of a Rolls-Royce engineer and a school lab technician. A writer from the age of six, with two unpublished novels in a drawer, she was stuck on a train in 1990 when Harry Potter walked, fully formed, into her mind.

Rowling spent the next five years constructing the plots of seven books, one for every year of his secondary school life. She began writing the first volume, *Harry Potter and the Philosopher's Stone*, in Portugal, where she was teaching English and had married a journalist. The marriage lasted barely a year, but produced baby Jessica.

Nobody except a wizard, it seems, could have predicted the phenomenal success of her novels, three of which are among the world's all-time best sellers and which have already spawned two hugely popular movies. In 2000, Rowling was awarded the Order of the British Empire during the Queen's birthday celebration.

In an interview with *Newsweek*, Rowling commented:

[When my daughter was six] I had told [her], "Not until you're seven [will I read you the Harry Potter books]," because I think a bright six-year-old can definitely manage it in terms of language, but in term of themes, things get increasingly scary and dark, and some six-year-olds are going to be disturbed by that. So for my own daughter, I said, "We're going to wait till you're seven."

But then she went to school, and she got completely mobbed. These older children were just talking to her endlessly about [the Harry Potter] stuff, and she didn't have a clue, and I thought it was unfair to keep her excluded from that, so we started reading them. . . ."

All the children in the books and all of the feelings in the books are based on my memories. They aren't based on anything my daughter has given me. It comes from inside me, my memories of being a child. And also, as I've said, so much of it was fixed before she was born. I think this is probably a good thing. I mean, we remember Christopher Robin, who was tormented till he died at the age of seventy-five by people taking the mickey out of him. That wasn't a smart thing to do, putting your child by name into the book, and his toys. I don't want Jessica to always be Harry Potter's sister. My worst fear, actually.

Later interviewed by *Readers Digest*, Rowling commented:

Children are a writer's dream. They are not interested in sales figures. They want to know why the plot works a certain way. They know about the books back to front, and talk about the characters as they though they were living, mutual friends of ours.

Surprised by Your Newborn

Catherine Zeta-Jones

Among the most beautiful actresses in the world today, Catherine Zeta-Jones was born to working-class parents in Wales. At the age of eleven, she starred in a London production of *Annie*, and by her mid-teens she was pursuing a full-time acting career. Zeta-Jones fared better on British and American TV than on the big screen during most of the 1990s, but in the 1998 Spielberg production *The Mask of Zorro*, she got her breakout role as heroine. Her subsequent films include *Entrapment, The Haunting*, *Traffic*, and the musical *Chicago*.

Zeta-Jones married *Traffic* co-star Michael Douglas in 2000, and their first child was born the following year. *People* weekly described the joyful event:

> Dylan Michael Douglas may have inherited his mother's thick, raven-colored hair. But it was a trait from his father's side that

leaped out at Catherine Zeta-Jones moments after her fiancé, Michael Douglas, cut the baby's umbilical cord at Los Angeles' Cedars-Sinai Medical Center at 5:52 P.M. on August 8th.

She screamed and said, "Look at that dimple," reports proud grandfather Kirk Douglas, age eighty-three. The next day, the acting family's patriarch saw it for himself. "It's even bigger than mine!" he brags. "That dimple made me feel especially close to him."

Later, Michael Douglas told the Spanish magazine *Brisas* that he was looking forward to becoming a second-time father. "When Cameron [his only child with ex-wife Diandra] was born, I was much more dedicated to my career. Now I can be a better husband, spend more time with my son, and also share in the success of my wife."

Talking with Your Child

Mel Gibson

Actor, director, and producer Mel Gibson immigrated as a child with his family from the New York City area to Sydney, Australia. After graduating from high school, he studied at the National Institute of Dramatic Art and made his screen debut in the low-budget film *Summer City* at the age of twenty-one. Starting in the late '70s, he gained awards for his dramatic roles in Australian movies including *Mad Max, Gallipoli, The Road Warrior*, and *The Year of Living Dangerously*. With the huge success of *Lethal Weapon* in 1987, Gibson became an established Hollywood star. Three sequels followed, together with such popular films as *Braveheart, Ransom, Payback, The Patriot, What Women Want, We Were Soldiers,* and *Signs*.

Once featured on the cover of *People* magazine as "the sexiest man alive," Gibson is now the father of seven children with Robyn Moore. In an interview with *McCall's,* he commented:

I don't want my children to be lulled into believing that life is a gravy train and that they don't have to work hard for their goals. My father is a hell of a man, and one of the things I learned from him is that you have to be responsible for your children. You can't abandon them to the forces of nature and hope that they'll turn out okay. Being a dad is part camp counselor and part military commander. You want them to have fun and grow up to be well-adjusted human beings. You also have to make sure they know it's a bad idea to do drugs and drive their dad's car at 150 miles per hour.

Children need guidance. They need to have some basic values and direction, to keep them free of bad temptations. But you can't behave like a dictator, or they'll turn into rebels. . . . The best thing I can do for my kids as a father is to provide them with some structure and some rational guideposts by which to live. Kids also need to grow up believing in their own identity and in their own particular interests. My kids know they can talk to me about anything that's going on in their lives, and I promise to listen with an open mind.

Denzel Washington

Graduating from Fordham University in the Bronx, Denzel Washington began appearing in dramatic TV and film roles during the early to mid-1980s. His breakthrough role came in 1987, with an Oscar-nominated supporting turn in *Cry Freedom*. Two years later, Washington took home the Academy Award for Best Supporting Actor in *Glory*. Among his popular films are *Training Day, Remember the Titans, Courage Under Fire*, and *Hurricane*, which won him a Golden Globe Award and an Academy Award nomination for Best Actor. He debuted as a director with *Antwone Fisher*. Married to singer-actress Pauletta Pearson, they have five children.

Washington, who serves as a spokesperson for the Boys & Girls Clubs of America, recounted for *Esquire* magazine:

My kids are getting the [family] history from my father-in-law. I'm so glad I had a chance before my father passed away to go out with him on the land, the property we owned. Him walking and showing us the boundaries, telling us the history: who was buried where, how they got the land, going back to the times when blacks couldn't own land and my great-great-grandfather married an Indian who could own land and bought it in her name. You know, two dollars an acre, a buck and a quarter an acre.

The lack of conversation between fathers and sons is one of the biggest deficits in our culture. It's a space that needs to be filled, and if we don't fill it, all kinds of dangerous stuff gets in there, somebody else gets their evil in there, and each generation is estranged from the next. We've got to start the struggle all over again with each new generation.

[My] kids probably had that kind of talk more with their grandfather than with me, because he knows what to say. I'm not as good at it as he is. And he's a guy that didn't really have parents around. The extended family was crucial to him.

The generations before were about letting things come out naturally. Evolving out of the moment as opposed to trying to make a moment, because they had more time. Time to sit on the porch, whittle wood, and the lesson—whatever—came out at the appropriate time. Maybe hours later. They didn't have to say: "Sit down and have this five minutes of wisdom, I gotta run."

Teaching Love for Reading

Laura Bush

The First Lady was a Texas schoolteacher and librarian for nine years before marrying in 1977. She and George W. met at a Dallas dinner party and wedded four months later. Their twin daughters, Jenna and Barbara (named for the girls' grandmothers) were born in 1981. During her husband's political career as governor, and subsequently in the White House, Laura Bush has emphasized reading achievement and improvement as a major goal for children today.

In an interview with Parenting.com, Laura Bush related:

We immediately started reading to our girls once they were home from the hospital and read with them as they grew older. Reading became a family activity. It's so important for parents to read and talk to their children. We loved the Maurice Sendak books like *Where the Wild Things Are* and *In the Night Kitchen*.

We read all of Dr. Seuss' books. *Goodnight Moon* was a special favorite when the girls were babies.

Television is no substitute for a parent. It doesn't help develop language skills; it's simply background noise. Children need to hear language early and often, directly from an adult.

The gift of learning begins with the gift of reading. Reading is the single most important skill children can learn. If you can read, you can be successful in every subject. Reading is also a necessary skill for a successful life. I encourage new parents to begin reading to their children as early as possible and as much as possible. Children who are read to learn two things: one, that reading is important; and, two, that they're important too.

Thinking About Fatherhood

Harrison Ford

A college dropout and struggling actor, Ford was a self-taught carpenter when, in 1973, he gained his first significant film role, in the low-budget comedy *American Graffiti*. It was a surprise commercial success, but more important for Ford, it introduced him to director George Lucas. Four years later, when making *Star Wars*, Lucas chose Ford—still doing carpentry work to earn a living—to play the renegade starship captain Han Solo. The rest, as they say, is history. Handsome, dynamic, and wise-cracking, Ford has carried this persona into such subsequent Lucas/Spielberg collaborations as *The Empire Strikes Back, Raiders of the Lost Ark* (in which he played a swashbuckling archaeologist), *Return of the Jedi*, and two Indiana Jones sequels. Over the years, Ford has expanded his immensely recognizable screen personality in such movies as *Witness, Working Girl, Patriot Games, Air Force One,* and *What Lies Beneath.*

The father of four children, Ford mused in a *Good Housekeeping* interview:

> My kids are as much out of control as anybody's. I struggle with it now, as much as I did when my first kids were born. I've got a thirty-three-year-old son. . . ."
>
> The ethical message in every movie I do is important, but I don't think they're appropriate for all ages in the same way. There might be a question of whether you'd want to take a seven-year-old to a movie like *Air Force One*. But, in fact, my then seven-year-old daughter showed no interest in it. She doesn't like that sort of thing. My eleven-year-old, on the other hand, loved it.

Bill Gates

The richest man in the world, Bill Gates is chairman and chief software architect for the Microsoft Corporation. Microsoft employs more than forty thousand people in sixty countries. The son of a wealthy Seattle attorney married to a schoolteacher, Gates was a precocious youngster who began programming computers at the age of thirteen. In 1973, he entered Harvard as a freshman, but left two years later to devote his energies to Microsoft, which he had founded with his childhood friend Paul Allen. Gates's books include *Business @ the Speed of*

Thought and *The Road Ahead*. In recent years, Gates, who now has two children, has turned increasingly to philanthropy and endowed the Bill and Melinda Gates Foundation with more than $21 billion to support initiatives in global health and learning.

In a *Time* cover-story interview, Gates commented:

Everyone starts out really capable. But as you grow and turn curious, either you get positive feedback by finding answers or you don't, and then this incredible potential that you have is discouraged. I was lucky. I always had a family and resources to get more and more answers.

Analytically, I would say that nature has done a good job of making child-raising more pleasure than pain, since that is necessary for a species to survive. But the experience goes beyond analytic description. . . . Evolution is many orders of magnitude ahead of mankind today in creating a complex system. I don't think it's irreconcilable to say we will understand the human mind someday and explain it in software-like terms, and also to say it is a creation that shouldn't be compared to software.

Religion has come around to the view that even things that can be explained scientifically can have an underlying purpose that goes beyond the science. Even though I am not religious, the amazement and wonder I have about the human mind is closer to religious awe than dispassionate analysis.

231

Tom Hanks

The star of such blockbusters as *Cast Away, Saving Private Ryan*, and *Forrest Gump*, Tom Hanks is reportedly the highest-paid actor in the world today. With his trusting, likeable screen persona in such hits as *Big, Philadelphia, Sleepless in Seattle*, and *You've Got Mail*—and the amiable voice of Woody in *Toy Story* and *Toy Story 2*—Hanks has been dubbed by critics a throwback to Hollywood's Golden Era brand of leading man. Besides winning numerous acting awards, he has been a successful director and producer, associated with *My Big Fat Greek Wedding* and the TV film mini-series *Band of Brothers* and *From the Earth to the Moon*.

The father of four children, Hanks observed in a *Time* interview:

My oldest son [actor Colin Hanks] is twenty-four. Throughout the vast majority of his youth and adolescence, I did not have a clue as to how to be a father or parent. It was at that point in my career where it was all about getting work. My daughter and he lived with their mom [Samantha Lewes]. With my younger kids [with wife Rita Wilson], now that I'm forty-five, it's of paramount importance to me that they have much more concrete security and stability. I have much more ability to provide that for them now. With my older kids, I simply wasn't able to do it.

Sylvester Stallone

Actor, director, and writer "Sly" Stallone grew up in New York City and briefly attended beauty school before gaining a scholarship at the American College in Switzerland. There he discovered a passion for acting, studying drama in Miami and his hometown. In 1974, Stallone's first substantial film role came, in *The Lords of Flatbush*. Two years later, he wrote and starred in the blockbuster *Rocky*, which propelled Stallone into the ranks of stardom—gaining him Academy Award nominations for Best Actor and Best Original Screenplay. He became most popular as an action hero in the 1980s and '90s for the four *Rocky* sequels, which he also directed, and his three *Rambo* movies. Though *Cliffhanger* and *Demolition Man* were successes at the box office, Stallone also gained critical praise for his later film *Cop Land*. He has five children, including three daughters from his present marriage to former model Jennifer Lavin.

For a *Good Housekeeping* interview, Stallone remarked:

Having daughters now, I can completely relate to the ferocity with which my character sets out to protect this kid. I'm excited to start playing the dad in movies, to use some of the emotions my family has stirred up in me. . . .

Boys are great, but you know, they break and kick and smash

233

things, and the dog's howling and the cat's hanging from a lamp. I highly recommend daughters. [But] girls do know how to cry. I can't handle it. They take one look at me and start bawling. I'm turning to [my wife] Jennifer, saying, "Honey, *why?*" But it's how they make their demands. . . .

When they were getting ready to wheel Sophia [at age two months] into heart surgery, this nurse turns to Jennifer and says, "Why don't you kiss your baby goodbye?" Not, "We'll see you in a few hours," or "We'll be back soon." But "Kiss your baby good-bye." Jennifer's knees started to buckle. I just turned to the nurse and said angrily, "Bad dialogue."

Thinking About Motherhood

Annette Bening

Annette Bening grew up in Topeka, Kansas, the daughter of an insurance salesman and a church singer. She trained at the American Conservatory Theater in San Francisco and received acclaim in the 1980s for her stage appearances. Bening debuted as a film actress in *The Great Outdoors*, a comedy. Subsequent movie roles included *Valmont, Bugsy*, and *The Grifters*, which earned her a Best Supporting Actress nomination. While starring opposite Warren Beatty in *Bugsy*, the two fell in love, and they married in 1992.

Raising four children together with Beatty, Bening has won acting praise for such films as *The American President, What Planet Are You From?*, and *American Beauty*, which garnered her an Academy Award nomination for Best Actress.

In a *Good Housekeeping* interview, Bening observed:

Many women talk to me about having kids—they're thinking about it or they've been waiting or something. Some people wait

 235

too long, and they can't get pregnant. I graduated from acting school after I got my degree from San Francisco State. When I realized I was the first girl in my acting class to have a baby—at thirty-two—it really gave me pause. Some of the men had gotten married and had children, but not the women. I thought, *Whoa!* Now, I tell other women, "Look, just do it—have a baby. Don't worry about it."

There's always this concern that motherhood is going to compromise your professional life. Of course, it totally changes your life. It does, in the most profound way. But I don't have any regrets. The older I get, the more I say, "Thank God my life turned out this way!"

When I turned forty last year, I felt very reflective. I felt like it was a time to sort of sit back and look at my life. And I really felt grateful that I had my kids. The most profound, gut-level feeling I had was *I've had three children. That's just incredible. Good for me.*

Celine Dion

The fourteenth child born to professional singers in Canada's French-speaking Quebec province, Celine Dion signed her first performing contract as a pre-teen. Her manager/producer René Angelil mortgaged his own home to finance Dion's debut album, *The Voice of God* (La Vox du bon Dieu), so certain was he of its success. By the age of eighteen, she had recorded nine French albums and won numerous awards. In 1994, following a long romance, she and Angelil married in Montreal. Three years later, Dion's singing voice became ubiquitous around the world when she sang the theme song, "My Heart Will Go On," for the blockbuster film *Titanic*. After years of fertility treatments, she gave birth to a boy, René-Charles, in 2001.

In an interview for *Redbook*, Dion confided:

> I never thought that my life would fall apart if I didn't have a child. But even so, I was waiting for it, looking for it, and making it part of my plans.
>
> I think it is such a privilege to give a baby its first home inside your body. [After my pregnancy was over] I found myself massaging my stomach gently. I miss him being in my body—stretching, hiccuping even. It was a wonderful, deep, loving, fulfilling feeling.

Jodie Foster

Starring in such popular films as *Contact* and *Silence of the Lambs*, Jodie Foster is among the world's leading actresses today. Raised in

Los Angeles by a financially hard-pressed mother, "little Jodie," as she was often called, depended on her siblings for nurturing. Her career was launched when, at the age of three, she successfully auditioned for Coppertone. By the age of fifteen, under her mother's skillful management, Jodie had appeared in more than fifty television shows including *Bonanza, Gunsmoke*, and *The Partridge Family*, and starred as a child actress in the movies *Alice Doesn't Live Here Anymore* and *Taxi Driver*, for which she won an Oscar nomination in 1976. After studying acting at Yale, Jodie appeared in a variety of well-received films including *Somersby, Nell, The Panic Room,* and *Home for the Holidays*, which she also directed.

In an interview for *Ladies Home Journal*, Foster commented:

Childbirth was the hardest thing to go through. [I] chose not to have an epidural because I thought it was the healthy way. It's a primal experience, and we don't have many of those. [As for breast-feeding], you expect everything to be so natural, but it takes a lot of work! . . .

Mine is not a traditional household, and my mom's wasn't either. Everybody is brought into this world with a different set of events. Traditions are not the point. The point is the amount of love, focus, and sensitivity that you can bring to the experience.

I can be very critical, of myself and other people. And you

know, Charlie is helping me with that. I would never want somebody else to be that way toward him. That's what having kids is about, they're there to show you all the crappy things you do that you have to stop doing. They are your therapy.

Diane Keaton

After rising to fame in a series of hit Woody Allen comedies including *Annie Hall, Sleeper*, and *Manhattan*, Keaton has enjoyed a successful career as an actress and director. Raised in Los Angeles, she studied acting at Manhattan's Neighborhood Playhouse School of the Theater, and she debuted as an understudy in *Hair*. Keaton's film hits include *Baby Boomer, Reds, The First Wives Club, Father of the Bride* and its sequel, and *Marvin's Room*, for which she won an Oscar nomination.

Unmarried despite high-profile liasons with Woody Allen, Warren Beatty, Al Pacino, and others, Keaton has two adopted children. She recently told *More* magazine in an interview:

We all need to share our personal history with somebody who has gone through it with us. It's a treasure in life.

[When my father died of a brain tumor] there was no way I could deny that life was moving on—the idea that a family could be postponed a second longer. I had to ask myself: "Are you, or aren't you?"

[My children] have changed me. I have my priorities in order, and the separation between work and personal life is profoundly different. . . .

I really hope I'm healthy, so that I can be vital in raising the kids.

Madonna (Ciccone)

Madonna is among the world's most popular entertainers. Her film credits include *Desperately Seeking Susan, Dick Tracy, Truth or Dare, Evita*, and *Swept Away*. Starting with her first album—*Madonna*—released in 1983 when she was twenty-five, her success has continued unabated. Since then, her hit singles have included "Material Girl," "Live to Tell," "Papa, Don't Preach," "Express Yourself," and "You'll See." Her most recent CDs, *Ray of Light* and *Music*, have been major successes, as has her recording company, Maverick Records.

Born in Grand Rapids, Michigan, in 1958, as a six-year-old Madonna suffered the loss of her mother, Madonna Fortin, to breast cancer. With six children in all, young Madonna's household was large and hard to manage, and a few years later, her father married their housekeeper, Joan Gustafson. After gaining a dance scholarship to the

University of Michigan in 1976, Madonna abruptly quit her studies, moved to New York City, and triumphed in her entertainment career goals.

In a wide-ranging interview for *Good Housekeeping*, Madonna commented:

"Is there ever a perfect time [to have a baby]? A baby's always going to interrupt something, isn't it?"

When asked if she is worried about protecting her one-year-old daughter, Madonna said, "It's the other way around. She protects me.

"I sing all the time to my daughter. Lots of silly songs that I make up. But don't ask me to repeat them."

Madonna doesn't mind offering some advice for first-time fathers in the delivery room. "Do everything you're told. Be a good cheerleader. And never, never say, 'It's not so bad.' Say 'You are almost there!' And say it a lot.

"From the moment I got pregnant, I started to look at life in a different way. Suddenly it was like, 'Oh my God, there's someone else to think about.' You cannot be an anarchist if you have children. I mean you can still be rebellious, but you always have to pause first.

"I haven't come to a place where I've said, 'Oh, no, I can't do that because it would upset Lola' at another date. But for instance, I was offered a play I thought was so dark. And I thought, I can't do a monologue about killing a child. I just can't. So there are lots of things that I can't—not *won't, can't*—do anymore because I have a kid. It's not on the level of, 'What will Lourdes think?' but about my own sensitivity now."

Michelle Pfeiffer

Over a twenty-year career, Michelle Pfeiffer has won popular and critical acclaim for such films as *I Am Sam, What Lies Beneath, Married to the Mob, One Fine Day, The Witches of Eastwick*, and *Dangerous Liasons*. Raised in southern California, Pfeiffer was a checkout-girl at a local supermarket, and reigned as Miss Orange County before being discovered by Hollywood. She has three children—two adopted children and the third with husband TV writer/producer David Kelley.

Interviewed by *Redbook*, Pfeiffer had this to say about motherhood:

I think that when you have your first child, you become so vulnerable in a way that you never were before you let many of your guards drop. I don't know why: maybe it's magic to be a mother. Having a daughter really changed my life, just completely, forever.

I think there's a kind of universal fear among women about

[the] first child—you begin to panic about being a good mother because you feel like you don't know anything.

I was pleasantly surprised that it came very naturally to me. I'm used to having really high expectations and then things falling short of those expectations.

So I was surprised that being a mother exceeded my expectations. The other thing is that it gets better and better. With each new stage, I think, Oh this is my favorite time.

Now, as they're getting older, they're becoming little people—their questions get more interesting and you get into conversations. So the bond [becomes] even stronger, and it's more complex, and it's more challenging. I just find motherhood very fulfilling. . . .

I think the worst thing is the sleep deprivation. It's just awful. And when I think about having another child, that's the one thing I worry about. I remember being so tired, especially with my son, because he was not a good sleeper. I'm just now getting caught up on my sleep. And I love to sleep.

Meg Ryan

Known as "America's Sweetheart" for starring in such romantic comedies as *When Harry Met Sally*, *Sleepless in Seattle*, *You've Got Mail*, and *Kate & Leopold*, Ryan grew up in suburban New York City.

When her mother left the family to pursue an acting career, her father, Harry, a high school teacher, was forced to raise the couple's four children. In her early twenties Ryan became a regular on the CBS soap opera *As the World Turns* before moving to Los Angeles. In 1989, she gained her first substantial film role in the hit *Top Gun*. She and ex-husband, actor Dennis Quaid, had one child, Jack, together. In an interview for *Redbook*, Ryan reflected:

> All of [motherhood] surprised me. It surprised me from the very first second I saw Jack. I'd believed that my pregnancy was a condition. It never computed. And there he was. Everyone made fun of me because I stared at him for months and months, not being able to believe he was real. He had a lot of hair when he was born, and they took him away and cleaned him up, and when they brought him back to me, he had a little part in it: I couldn't get over it. He knew how to breast-feed and I didn't.
>
> Having a child is a lot of work, and sometimes I feel like there's always someone I am disappointing. I was really unprepared for how great it was going to be.
>
> Becoming a mother gave me the confidence to move into other areas. I felt so capable as a mother, which is something I never thought I would do. I felt like, "I can do this." I like that Jack has a routine, which I never had. Now because I have one—because of him—I thrive on it.

It's so fundamental, what you're doing for another person. And you're able to do it even though it takes a lot of work. I wouldn't have thought of myself as a person who could guide anybody. And then it turned out that I can. Not that I'm perfect. But it turns out I have answers to some of these questions. And if I don't, I can say: "You know, I have that question too."

Maria Shriver

A contributing anchor for *Dateline* on NBC and contributing correspondent for MSNBC, Maria Shriver has been active in the broadcasting news field for more than fifteen years. Her recent best-sellers have included the children's book *What's Heaven?* and *Ten Things I Wish I'd Known Before I Went Out into the Real World*. In an interview for *Good Housekeeping*, Shriver offered these thoughts:

Barbara Walters, who was a single mother, gave me a lot of advice when I was struggling with my job. She was actually very blunt. She said, "Look, your kids are only young once. Don't do what I did. Take your time. You're talented. You're going to be okay. If you need to work less, they'll keep you [at your work].

Growing up with four brothers, I would always think: *Gee, I wish I were a guy*. But once I had children, I was so proud to be a woman. I feel this mother "sisterhood," that I'm really in a really cool thing. It opens up a whole new world of interesting challenges. Even though it ended up being much more difficult than I ever thought. My mother never gave me the sense that she was having to work hard at it. So I was shocked. I was like, "God, this is so hard!"

I believe everyone should find whatever works to get them through the day. Do whatever you can do. If your dining-room ritual is five minutes, God bless you. I look at some mothers doing that soccer thing, cooking, and sewing the clothes, and I feel bad. At Halloween, my daughters were coming in saying, "So-and-so's mother is *making* her costume, and I thought, *Oh, God, I'm so bad!* They'll say, "So-and-so's mother serves hot lunch every day. You don't." It's important not to compare ourselves to anyone else.

Uma Thurman

Nominated for a Best Supporting Actress Academy Award in *Pulp Fiction*, Uma (named after a Hindu deity) has been appearing in films since the age of seventeen. The daughter of a Buddhist scholar/monk father and psychotherapist (and former Swedish model) mother, Uma grew up in Massachussetts and debuted in *Kiss Daddy Goodnight*, a low-budget thriller. Her best-known movies include *Batman and Robin, Les Misérables, The Avengers*, and *Gattaca*. In 1998, Uma married *Gattaca* co-star Ethan Hawke, with whom she now has two children.

For a feature article in *Rosie* magazine, Thurman confided:

When you have a child—if that doesn't ground you, nothing will. I feel so protective of my daughter and her generation. The thing is, raising a child is also raising a citizen. I guess that's why I'm so committed to [my friend] Julie and Room to Grow. I hope my daughter becomes the type of person who doesn't take her life for granted and is generous.

Many of the mothers I know spend their days dragging their children to endless classes. I take my daughter to a few classes, but you can't get into that competitiveness stuff. That's really too crazy. Actually, that's why it makes so much sense to me to come here [Room to Grow]. These are real issues. . . .

I feel very moved by children. They are innocent and helpless. Their unnecessary suffering takes your breath away. You can't be a mother and not think about the world your children's contemporaries are coming into. . . .

[My childbirth] was a pretty scary thing. When you think of something that big inside you, and then have to get it out of you, it's either going to be the knife or you that's going to get it out. I was in labor for a very long time—about eighteen hours. [The drug] Pitocin is what pushed me over the edge, because it artificially stimulates you. Ethan was there for all of it, and he got high accolades from the doctor. But we don't talk about it. Very few things are personal to me. The birth and the child are very difficult to keep private, because people can ask and it's very difficult to shut down a conversation about your baby.

Witnessing the Birth

Andrea Bocelli

Blindness did not stop Andrea Bocelli's passion and drive for music, and for life. He took inspiration from the long line of immortal Italian tenors, and as a teenager was the victor in a number of music competitions. Yet he was uncertain of his chances at a music career—instead, he studied law. Bocelli attracted the attention and aid of Luciano Pavarotti, and by 1996 he had an international hit—his recording of "Time to Say Goodbye," a duet with Sarah Brightman. His two subsequent albums, *Romanza* and *Aria*, topped classical and crossover charts worldwide, and fans pack the stadiums during his concert appearances.

In *Andrea Bocelli, A Celebration*, biographer Antonia Felix recounted:

Andrea was the picture of the nervous father while Enrica was in labor with Matteo. Pacing back and forth on a terrace of the

Lotti Hospital in Pontedara, he couldn't bear to experience his wife in pain. "It is difficult and sad to witness suffering," he said. "The joy to know that something wonderful is happening is not enough. This is why I did not have the courage to stay with Enrica in the delivery room. I had to wait outside nervously."

To insure the privacy of his wife and himself while Enrica was at the hospital, Andrea hired five security specialists from an international security company called La First. They sealed off the clinic to everyone except staff and close family members of the other patients, with Bocelli's elite guard standing watch at the exits and outside Enrica's room. With her mother, Giuliana, at her side, Enrica gave birth to Matteo at one-thirty that afternoon. The local newspaper carried the news in blissful detail.

Just as he had done with Amos, Andrea held the newborn Matteo in his arms immediately after he was born. "I was overcome with happiness, love, and tenderness. . . . Right after he was washed, I studied him with my hands: his downy little head, his little nose, everything on the tiny body," he recalled.

Andrea explained that he sees his children with his hands. "As I once could see for some years, after, I know what most things look like," he said. "If I don't know it, then I feel it with my hands. I always say that I look with my hands. I know precisely how Amos looks, and I also know the looks of my second son. How I can see with my hands I can't explain. . . ."

"There is nothing that makes me happier than being a father," Andrea said. His family is "my reason for living, my drug, my oxygen. I feel I need them more than they need me. These children represent everything to me. I want to surpass myself so they will be proud of me, so that they can carry the torch, whatever career they choose. I want to be an example, a model and a guiding light for them."

Michael Caine

Exemplar of British cool in the swinging '60s and action star in the '70s, Michael Caine was knighted into official respectability in 1993. The Cockney son of a fish-porter and a charwoman, his best-known films include *The Ipress File, Alfie, Sleuth, Educating Rita, Dirty Rotten Scoundrels*, and, more recently, *Austin Powers in Goldmember* and *The Cider House Rules*, for which Caine won his second Best Supporting Actor Academy Award. He remains one of the most established performers in Hollywood, serving as a role model for actors and filmmakers alike.

In his memoir, *What's It's All About?* Caine jovially recalled:

Shakira was already in the first throes of birth and looked as if she could manage without me if I passed out. I was led to the head of the bed and given my wife's hand and told to do my job, which was to push with her. This I did for another hour and a half with such enthusiasm that I knew I was setting myself up for a hernia or piles in later life. I had a quick look around to see which was the best direction to fall if I did keel over, and saw with some satisfaction that there was enough space quite close by on the floor that could safely contain my inert body without disturbing the proceedings if the worst came to the worst.

After a while I grew used to the atmosphere and felt that I was going to be all right. Everything was going fine. We were in time with our pushes, she would smile up at me occasionally between bouts and it was at those times that I felt so glad that I had decided to be with her. Suddenly, with a cry of enthusiasm, Gordon Bourne grabbed a pair of scissors and started to snip at something at the other end. I could not see what he was doing, and it was here that my imagination ran riot and I nearly collapsed.

I was just about to stagger out when he held up one hand and in it was a lock of hair. "It's got a lot of hair and it's black," he announced triumphantly. Followed by "We're nearly there now. Just a few more pushes from the two of you," he said, urging us on. Together we gave our final heaves and out it came, bawling its head off immediately. "It's a girl." I didn't care what sex it was. I was waiting for the next report. "And she's perfect."

I looked at my child as the doctor held her up and she was truly perfect. I almost cried with relief and happiness.

John Denver

John Denver (born Henry John Deutschendorf Jr.) was a musical icon of the 1970s. Writing/performing such hit ballads as "Leaving on a Jet Plane," "Take Me Home, Country Roads," "Rocky Mountain High," and "Sunshine on My Shoulders," he garnered fourteen gold albums and countless awards around the world. With a humanitarian and environmentalist message in his songs, in 1976 Denver co-founded the Windstar Foundation, devoted to environmental research and education. He also served as a member of the Presidential Commission on World and Domestic Hunger. At the age of fifty-three, Denver was killed piloting his single-engine plane off the San Francisco coastline.

In *Take Me Home: An Autobiography*, published just three years before his death, Denver offered this fatherly remembrance:

If music is possibility given form, then Jesse Belle's birth was pure music. In fact, during early labor, part of me was still detached, as if I were there as a privileged spectator, having an aesthetic experience watching Cassie and her mother, who were wonderful to see together in that situation. Her mother was a great comfort and Cassie was just remarkable in response. I tried to set the rhythm for the breathing. . . .

The labor continued for eight hours. Then all at once, or so it seemed, the midwife turned to me and asked, "Do you want to deliver the baby?" I didn't have time to think about it, I just got the gloves on and I got down at the foot of the delivery table. The baby's head was about to emerge. I'd never seen a live birth. All I knew was what I had heard, and the technical descriptions didn't compute in my mind. Didn't click. Now here we were and I could feel the baby moving; I could hear its heartbeat, see it there about to be born. It was a real miracle. . . .

Finally, I put the baby on Carrie's bosom. I thought I could start to step back from it and take pleasure in seeing mother and child in repose, but it was too soon. The midwife had to attend to Cassie and handed the baby back to me. This time, I went over to a corner and sat down, baby Jesse Belle in my arms. How was it, I wondered, that for centuries men could absent themselves from this whole process? It was beyond me how they could accept not being allowed to participate in this incredible voyage. At that moment, I couldn't conceive that there was anywhere else to be. Just then Jesse Belle opened up the biggest blue eyes you've ever seen—they still are—and we just looked at each other. Then I sang to her and talked to her and, finally finding release, I cried all over her.

Frank McCourt

The Pulitzer Prize–winning author of memoirs *Angela's Ashes* and *'Tis*, Frank McCourt grew up in Ireland and returned to New York City, his birthplace, at the age of nineteen. He held a string of casual jobs, was an avid reader, and eventually became a high school English teacher. After retiring from teaching, McCourt performed with his brother Malachy in a two-man show, *A Couple of Blaguards*, about their Irish youth. He was already in his sixties when *Angela's Ashes*, his first book, became a best-seller initially in the United States, then in Ireland, the rest of Europe, and around the world—as well as an acclaimed film.

For his second memoir *'Tis*, McCourt reminisced:

In 1971 my daughter Maggie was born at Unity Hospital in the Bedford-Stuyvesant area of Brooklyn. There would be no problem taking home the right infant since she seemed to be the only white one in the nursery.

Alberta wanted a natural Lamaze childbirth, but the doctors and nurses at Unity Hospital had no patience with middle-class women and their peculiarities. They had no time for this woman and her breathing exercises and jabbed her with an anaesthetic to hasten the birth. Instead, that slowed the rhythm so much the impatient doctor clamped forceps on Maggie's head and yanked her from her mother's womb and I wanted to punch him for the flatness he left on her temples.

The nurse took the child to a corner to clean and wash her and when she finished beckoned that I might now see my daughter with her red astonished face and her black feet.

The soles of her feet were black. God, what kind of birthmark have you inflicted on my child? I couldn't say anything to the nurse because she was black and might be offended that I didn't find my daughter's black feet attractive. I had a vision of my child as a young woman lolling on a beach, lovely in a bathing suit but forced to wear socks to conceal her disfigurement. . . .

Alberta was wheeled back to her room and I called Malachy to tell him the good news, that a child had been born but that she was afflicted with black feet. He laughed at me and told me I was an [idiot], that the nurse probably took footprints instead of fingerprints. . . . Malachy was right. There was no hangover, only delight that a little child in Brooklyn had my name and I'd have a lifetime watching her grow.

Christopher Reeve

Raised in New York City and educated at Cornell, Christopher Reeve is undoubtedly best known for his movie role as *Superman*. His other popular films include the cult-classic romantic fantasy *Somewhere in Time* and *Rear Window*. As a result of a horseback riding accident in 1998, Reeve suffered major neurological trauma and injury. But in addition to making remarkable personal improvement, he has become a major advocate for Americans who are disabled and their medical and economic rights. Reeve has authored two well-received books, *Nothing Is Impossible*, and the earlier memoir, *Still Me*, in which he fondly recalled:

> The real highlight of 1979—in fact the highlight of my entire life up to that point—was the birth of my son Matthew on December 20th.
>
> He was born at the Welbeck Street Clinic in Mayfair. Gae had checked in the previous night, and I had stayed with her, expecting Matthew's imminent arrival. But by ten o'clock the next morning, the doctors thought it might be false labor and even considered sending us home. Laraine Ashton and her father invited me to lunch. We agreed that I would check back at the clinic in the early afternoon.

We had just started the main course when the headwaiter raced to our table with the message that the baby would be born any moment. I ran out of the restaurant, and miraculously there was a cab waiting right outside the door. (Usually it's so difficult to find a cab in London when you need one that you call to book in advance. Finding one right in front of a restaurant seemed like a sign from the gods.)

I told the driver that I would pay him double the meter if he would take me to Welbeck Street as quickly as possible without getting us killed. He was more than happy to oblige, but I'll always remember his calming remark, "Relax, Guv, when my first was born I was at the track. Much nicer place to be." He continued to chat pleasantly about fathers and sons while driving at breakneck speed toward Mayfair, sometimes literally driving on the sidewalk.

I took surviving the ride as another sign from the gods. I rushed up the stairs and into Gae's room just as Matthew appeared. I had the privilege of handing him to Gae, who was crying from both exhaustion and joy. Instead of bawling at the top of his lungs, as I had expected, Matthew snuggled in quietly and drifted off to sleep. But just before he dozed off, he opened one eye and looked right at me.

It seemed to me that he was asking, "Who are you?" And then, satisfied that I was meant to be there, he fell asleep. I think that look of complete acceptance from my first child within moments of his birth somehow taught me the most important lesson about being a parent: unconditional love is everything.

Isaac Stern

In a career spanning more than sixty years, Stern has appeared on the world's most prestigious concert stages, guided the careers of countless young musicians, and energetically advanced the arts internationally. He was born in a small town in Russia, but immigrated as a tot with his family to San Francisco, debuting professionally in 1933, at the age of thirteen. As president of Carnegie Hall for more than thirty-five years, Stern spearheaded the drives to save the hall from demolition in 1960 and to restore it in 1986. The recipient of the Presidential Medal of Honor, Stern has won governmental awards from France, Israel, and Japan, and is among the most recorded classical musicians of our time.

In his memoir *My First 79 Years*, the famous violinist warmly recalled:

I was on tour in Russia when our first child was born in 1956. When our second child, Michael, was due to be born, in 1959, the pediatrician, Dr. Jascha Rowe, was so busy bringing him into

THE BOOK OF BABY LOVE

the world that he could call me only after the birth. But with our third child, David, Dr. Rowe got to me in time, and I was in the delivery room, gowned and face-masked.

To be able to give his mother moral and physical support; to see this new lump of flesh emerge, turn from its fetal position, open its arms, give a cry, and instantly become a sentient human being—I will never forget that moment, nor forget the closeness it made me feel, not only to this third child but to the two others. It was a vision of nature in its rawest and most glorious moment. I urge every father-to-be to make every effort to realize that moment.

Harry Truman

Harry Truman's presidency was marked by such momentous events as the dropping of the atomic bomb on Japan, the Allied victory in World War II, the start of the Cold War, and the Korean War. During the decades since Truman's administration ended in 1952, historians have come to regard him with increasing respect. As a father, Truman was extremely close to his only child, Margaret.

In David McCullough's award-winning biography, *Truman*, the author recounted:

The arrival of the baby, in the midst of a snowstorm, Sunday, February 17, 1924, was, with the exception of his wedding day, the biggest event of Harry Truman's life thus far, and the one bright moment in what otherwise was to be a bad year for him.

He had urged Bess to go out to a hospital. She and her mother insisted the baby be born at home. Out of superstition that too much advance fuss could again bring disappointment, there was not even a crib or cradle at hand. The baby would spend the first days of life on pillows in a bureau drawer.

About noon, Harry was told to call the doctor . . . a big, red-faced man remembered for his huge hands—"hands as big as a frying pan"—who came in covered with snow and went directly upstairs. A practical nurse, Edna Kinnaman, arrived soon after and would remember Mrs. Wallace [Bess' mother] and Harry waiting patiently through the afternoon in the upstairs hall, the very proper Mrs. Wallace seated on a cedar chest, Harry in a chair looking amazingly composed.

Bess, according to Nurse Kinnaman, "got along beautifully." It was a normal birth. The baby, a girl, weighed 7½ pounds. "We didn't have to announce it [when the baby arrived] . . . because they heard her cry and the grandmother and daddy came into the room." It was five o'clock. Harry called his mother and sister and told them the name would be Mary Margaret, after Mary

Jane and Mrs. Wallace. The wife of a friend who saw him soon afterward said "his face just beamed."

Peter Ustinov

Among Britain's most venerable actors, Peter Ustinov was born in England to parents of Russian lineage. He trained at the London Theatre Studio and began writing sketches and performing on stage at the age of seventeen. In 1941, Ustinov debuted on the big screen with his role in *One of Our Planes Is Missing*, and during the 1950s and '60s he starred in *Quo Vadis, Spartacus, Billy Budd, Topkapi*, and *Viva Max!* His later film successes include *Logan's Run, The Thief of Baghdad, Death on the Nile*, and *Lorenzo's Oil*.

In his memoir, *Dear Me*, Ustinov reminisced:

On July 25th, 1945, our daughter was born at the Woolavington wing of the Middlesex Hospital in London. She is now a creature of grace and charm, with an expression ever youthful and delicate. Then she was entirely bald. A physical feature she retained for an alarming length of time, and her face had about as much of the secrecy and doggedness of a Soviet Field Marshal. As I looked at her, trying to kindle feelings of paternity, which are entirely intellectual with such tiny children, she stared straight back at me with surprisingly steady blue eyes as though awaiting a complete confession.

My confusion at this inquisitorial gaze was checked by the remark of a swarthy gentleman next to me, who was gazing for the first time at his daughter, in the next slot on the hors d'ouevre tray. His girl had a full head of black hair and carried an expression of irritation on her small features, as though she couldn't get her castanets to click. "They're all much of a much-ness, aren't they?" he said, heaving with fraternity.

Working During Pregnancy

Diana Ross

Diana Ross, a superstar in today's entertainment world, grew up in lower-middle-class 1950s Detroit. Showing early talent, she became lead singer for the female trio known as the Supremes and by her early twenties was one of Motown Record's most successful performers. Diana went solo in 1969 and immediately gained new hits with "Someday, We'll Be Together," "Reach Out and Touch Somebody's Hand," and "Ain't No Mountain High Enough." As an actress, her popular movies have included *Lady Sings the Blues* (in which she portrayed singer Billie Holiday) and *Mahogany*. Through live and televised concerts, Diana Ross has retained an enthusiastic following.

In a memoir entitled *Secrets of a Sparrow*, she recalled:

When I made the decision to do the movie, I had just become pregnant with my first baby, Rhonda. I had always wanted to be a mother, and I remember thinking, "I can't do this film because I'm going to have a baby." The film kept getting delayed, as they often do, and I used my nine months of pregnancy to read whatever I could about Billie Holiday, about drugs, and about drug addiction. I studied everything related to the film that I could get my hands on. This was a perfect time for research. During each of my pregnancies, I have worked through my sixth month. I never really stop.

As often happens with first pregnancies, I was sick a lot, and I didn't go out very much. I took this further opportunity to study, read, and listen to Billie Holiday's music.

Writing to a Baby Nephew

John F. Kennedy

John F. Kennedy was very much enamored of his two children, Caroline and John Jr. In January 1961, when the forty-three-year-old Kennedy took office as president, his daughter was a toddler and his son newly born. Later, President Theodore Roosevelt's daughter Alice Roosevelt Longworth was visiting the Kennedys at the White House and observed how casually the children ran around the family's living quarters on the second floor. She remarked, "This is just the way it was when I lived here."

Caroline made it a ritual to walk with her father downstairs to work every morning. She called him Silly Daddy and he called her Buttons. She had a way of parking herself on his lap during breakfast meetings with the presidential staff. He always let her stay. Or Caroline might walk imperiously into a meeting to announce in a loud and clear voice, "Mommy wants you!"

On one occasion, Joseph Kennedy teasingly said to his son, the president, "Caroline's very bright, smarter than you were at that age."

"Yes, she is," was the instant quip, "but look who she has for a father!"

Upon the birth of a new nephew, Kennedy addressed this humorous letter to him:

Welcome, to the youngest member of the clan. Your entrance is timely, as we need a new left end on the team. Here's hoping that you do not acquire the political assets of your parents, the prolific qualities of your godfather [Bobby], or the problems of your uncle.

Writing to Your Baby

Richard Harding Davis

A pioneer in the long line of American foreign correspondents was Richard Harding Davis, who reported wars throughout the world. In October 1915, Davis was on his way to the horrific Ardennes front when he composed this letter to his daughter, Hope, born the previous January:

> So many weeks have passed since I saw you that by now you are able to read this without your mother looking over your shoulder and helping you with the big words. I have six sets of pictures of you. Every day I take them down and change them. Those your dear mother put in glass frames I do not change. Also, I have all the sweet fruits and chocolates and red bananas. How good of you to think of just the things your father likes. Some of them I gave to a little boy and girl. I play with them because soon my

daughter will be as big. They have no mother like yours—so loving, so tender, so unselfish, and thoughtful. If she is reading this, kiss her for me. . . .

Be very good. Do not bump yourself. Do not eat matches. Do not play with scissors or cats. Do not forget your dad. Sleep when your mother wishes it. Love us both. Try to know how we love you. *That* you will never learn. Goodnight and God keep you, and bless you.

Mark Twain

Mark Twain was enamored with his three daughters—Olivia Susan, Clara, and Jean. In her lively memoir, *My Father Mark Twain*, which middle-child Clara wrote in middle age, she shared this delightful paternal letter. Though undated, it was undoubtedly composed in the mid-1870s:

LETTER FROM SANTA

My dear Susie Clemens,

I have received and read all the letters which you and your little sister have written me by the hand of your mother and nurses; I have also read those which you little people have written me with your own hands—for although you did not use any characters that are in grown peoples' alphabet, you used the characters that all children in all lands on earth and in the twinkling stars use; and as all my subjects in the moon are children and use no character but that, you will easily understand that I can read your and your baby sister's jagged and fantastic marks without any trouble at all.

But I had trouble with those letters which you dictated through your mother and the nurses, for I am a foreigner and cannot read English writing well. You will find that I made no mistakes about the things which you and the baby ordered in your *own* letters. I went down your chimney at midnight when you were asleep and delivered them all myself, and kissed both of you, too, because you are good children, well-trained, nice-mannered, and about the most obedient little people I ever saw.

Sources

Aaron, Henry. *I Had a Hammer, the Hank Aaron Story*. New York: Harper-Collins, 1991.

Abbott, Denise. "Celebrity Close-Up." *McCall's*, March 2001, 16–19.

Adams, Abigail and John. *The Book of Abigail and John, Selected Letters of the Adams Family, 1762–1784*. Edited and with an introduction by L.H. Butterfield, Marc Friedlander, and Mary-Jo Kline. Cambridge: Harvard University Press, 1975.

Adler, Bill. *Kids' Letters to President Kennedy*. New York: Morrow, 1961.

———. *Motherhood, a Celebration*. New York: Carroll & Graf, 1987.

Albanese, Andrew, and Brandon Trissler. *Graduation Day, The Best of America's Commencement Speeches*. New York: Morrow, 1998.

Alcott, Bronson. *The Journals of Bronson Alcott*. Selected and edited by Odell Shepard. Boston: Little, Brown, 1938.

Allen, Tim. *Don't Stand Too Close to a Naked Man*. New York: Hyperion, 1994.

Anderson, Loni. *My Life in High Heels*. New York: Morrow, 1995.

Angelou, Maya. *I Know Why the Caged Bird Sings*. New York: Bantam, 1993.

Bacall, Lauren. *Now*. New York: Knopf, 1994.

Ball, Lucille. *Love, Lucy*. New York: Putnam's Sons, 1996.

"Barbara Walters." *Ladies Home Journal*, May 2001, 104–105, 165–166.

Barr, Roseanne. *Roseanne, My Life as a Woman*. New York: Harper & Row, 1987.

Barry, Dave. *Dave Barry Is Not Making This Up*. New York: Crown, 1994.

Bedell, Madelon. *The Alcotts, Biography of a Family*. New York: Clarkson N. Potter, 1980.

Blackman, Ann. *Seasons of Her Life: A Biography of Madeleine Albright*. New York: Scribner, 1998.

Blake, William. *Selected Poems*. Edited by Peter Butter. London: Everyman, 1993.

Bouquet, Tim. "The Wizard Behind Harry Potter." *Reader's Digest*, December 2000, 96–101.

Brochu, Jim. *Lucy in the Afternoon, An Intimate Portrait Of Lucille Ball*. New York: Morrow, 1990.

"By Zeus, It's a Boy!" *People*, September 17, 2001, 196–197.

Caine, Michael. *What's It All About?* New York: Random House, 1992.

Caldicott, Helen. *A Desperate Passion, an Autobiography*. New York: Norton, 1997.

Cher. *The First Time*. New York: Simon & Schuster, 1998.

Christie, Agatha. *An Autobiography*. New York: Dodd, Mead, 1977.

Clemens, Clara. *My Father, Mark Twain*. New York: Harper & Brothers, 1931.

Clemens, Samuel. *The Autobiography of Mark Twain*. Arranged and edited by Charles Neider. New York: Harper & Row, 1959.

Coleridge, Samuel. *Poems*. Edited by John Beer. London: Everyman, 1995.

Collins, Judy. *Singing Lessons: A Memoir of Love, Loss, Hope, and Healing*. New York: Pocket Books, 1998.

Corliss, Richard. "Playtime for Gonzo." *Time*, December 28, 1987, volume 130, number 26, 75–77.

Cosby, Bill. *Fatherhood*. Garden City, New York: Doubleday, 1986.

Coyne, Kate. "Sylvester Stallone Father Figure." *Good Housekeeping*, November 2000, 113–114.

———. "Kelly Cuts Loose." *Good Housekeeping*, March 2002, 106–108.

———. "Faith Hill Fesses Up." *Good Housekeeping*, April 2002, 94–97, 170.

Denver, John. *Take Me Home*. New York: Harmony, 1994.

Dickens, Charles. *The Letters of Charles Dickens, Volume One, 1820–1839*. Edited by Madeline House and Graham Storey. Oxford: Clarendon, 1965.

Draisin, LaVera. "Birth, Creation Stories, and the Spiritual Journey: Teachings from the Navajo and the Kabbalah." In Edward Hoffman (Editor), *Opening the Inner Gates*. Boston: Shambhala, 1995.

Dukakis, Kitty. *Now You Know*. New York: Simon & Schuster, 1990.

Emerson, Lidian Jackson. *The Selected Letters of Lidian Jackson Emerson*. Edited with an introduction by Delores Bird Carpenter. Columbia: University of Missouri Press, 1987.

Emerson, Ralph Waldo. *Emerson in His Journals*. Edited by Joel Porte. Cambridge: Harvard University Press, 1982.

———. *Letters from Ralph Waldo Emerson to a Friend, 1838–1853*. Edited by Charles Eliot Norton. Boston: Houghton Mifflin, 1899.

Farrow, Mia. *What Falls Away: A Memoir*. Garden City, N.Y.: Doubleday, 1997.

Felix, Antonia. *Andrea Bocelli, a Celebration*. New York: St. Martin's Press, 2000.

Fonda, Peter. *My Life*, as told to Howard Teichmann. New York: New American Library, 1981.

Fox, Michael J. *Lucky Man*. New York: Hyperion, 2002.

Franklin, Aretha. *Aretha, From These Roots*. New York: Villard, 1999.

Freud, Sigmund. *Letters of Sigmund Freud*. Selected and edited by Ernest L. Freud. Translated by Tania and James Stern. New York: Dover, 1992.

Fuller, Graham. "The Not-So-Rough-Cut." *Interview*, January 2000, volume 30, i1, 44–49.

Gardner, Ava. *My Story*. New York: Bantam, 1990.

Gerosa, Melina. "Fascinating Mom." *Ladies Home Journal*, January 2001, 89–91.

Gifford, Kathie Lee. *I Can't Believe I Said That! An Autobiography with Jim Jerome*. New York: Pocket, 1992.

Gliatto, Tom, Mark Dagostino, Caroline Howard, Ellen Mazzo, and Pamela Warrick. "Yada Yada Yada: Jerry Seinfeld Enjoys Serenity Now as an Author, Documentary Star, Husband and New Father. You've Got to See the Baby!" *People*, October 21, 2002, volume 58, i17, 86–92.

Graham, Katharine. *Personal History*. New York: Vintage, 1997.

Griffin, Nancy. "Agent Provocateur." *Los Angeles Magazine*, November 2000, volume 45, i11, 108–111.

Hoffman, Edward. *The Book of Birthday Wishes*. New York: Kensington, 2001.

———. *The Book of Fathers' Wisdom: Paternal Advice from Moses to Bob Dylan*. Secaucus, N.J.: Carol Publishing, 1997.

Hoffman, Edward, and Marcella Bakur Weiner. *The Book of Love Compatibility*. Novato, Calif.: New World Library, 2002.

Hotchner, A. E. *Sophia, Living and Loving, Her Own Story*. New York: Morrow, 1979.

Isaacson, Walter. "In Search of the Real Bill Gates." *Time*, January 13, 1997, number 2, 44–55.

Jansenn, Jan. "Mel Gibson's Lessons for Life." *McCall's*, August 2000, 42–44.

Jones, Evan. *The Father: Letters to Sons and Daughters*. London: Andre Deutsch, 1960.

Jones, Malcolm. "The Return of Harry Potter." *Entertainment Weekly*, August 11, 2000, i554, 28–30.

Jong, Erica. *Fear of Fifty, A Memoir*. New York: HarperPerennial, 1995.

Kim, Namjo. *Selected Poems of Namjo Kim*. Translated by David R. McCann and Hyuanjae Yee Sallee. Ithaca: Cornell University East Asia Program, 1993.

King, Coretta Scott. *My Life with Martin Luther King, Jr.* New York: Holt, Rinehart and Winston, 1969.

Lessing, Doris. *Under My Skin*. New York: HarperCollins, 1994.

Lincoln, Mary Todd. *Mary Todd Lincoln, Her Life and Letters*. Edited by Justin G. Turner and Linda Levitt Turner. New York: Knopf, 1972.

McCourt, Frank. *'Tis, a Memoir*. New York: Scribner, 1999.

McCullough, David. *Truman*. New York: Simon & Schuster, 1996.

"Mom to Mom." *Rosie*, October 2001, 62–70.

Nash, Alanna. "Marvelous Meg." *Good Housekeeping*, July 1998, volume 227, number 1, 96–99.

Norment, Lynn. "You Can Have It All." *Ebony*, May 2002, 46–48, 50, 170.

O'Brien, Elizabeth. "Mother's Day." *People*, January 29, 2001, 59.

O'Donnell, Rosie. *Find Me*. New York: Warner, 2002.

Osborne, Claire G. (Editor). *The Unique Voice of Hillary Rodham Clinton: A Portrait in Her Own Words*. New York: Avon, 1997.

Powell, Colin. *My American Journey*. New York: Random House, 1995.

Powell, Joanna. "Pierce Brosnan." *People*, November 26, 2001.

———. "Sally Field: 'I Want to Do So Much!' " *Good Housekeeping*, June 2001, 95–98, 103–104.

———. "Harrison's Passions." *Good Housekeeping*, October 1999, volume 229, i4, 120–126.

———. "There Was a Lot of Loss Around." *Good Housekeeping*, March 1999, 104–108.

Reeve, Christopher. *Still Me*. New York: Random House, 1998.

Reiser, Paul. *Babyhood*. New York: Avon, 1997.

Roosevelt, Eleanor. *This Is My Story*. Garden City, N.Y.: Doubleday, 1939.

Roosevelt, Theodore. *The Selected Letters of Theodore Roosevelt*. Edited by H. W. Brands. New York: Cooper Square Press, 2001.

Rosenberg, Judith. (Editor). *A Question of Balance: Artists and Writers on Motherhood*. Watsonville, Calif.: Papier-Mache Press, 1995.

Ross, Diana. *Secrets of a Sparrow*. New York: Villard, 1993.

Russell, Lisa. "Eager Weaver." *People*, May 22, 1995, volume 43, number 20, 98.

Schneerson, Menachem Mendel. *Toward a Meaningful Life*. Adapted by Simon Jacobson. New York: Morrow, 1995.

Seymour, Jane. *Two at a Time, Having Twins: The Journey Through Pregnancy and Birth*. New York: Pocket Books, 2001.

SOURCES

Shapiro, Marc. *Behind Sad Eyes, The Life of George Harrison*. New York: St. Martin's Press, 2002.

Shepherd, Cybill. *Cybill Disobedience*. New York: HarperCollins, 2000.

Slick, Grace. *Somebody to Love? A Rock-and-Roll Memoir*. New York: Warner, 1998.

Smith, Liz. "The Meryl Streep Nobody Knows." *Good Housekeeping*, September 1998, volume 227, number 3, 94–100.

———. "What She Did for Love." *Good Housekeeping*, March 2000, 83–85m 108.

———. "Madonna Grows Up." *Good Housekeeping*, April 2000, 104–106, 178–180.

———. "Nicole Kidman on Life After Divorce and Fighting for What's Fair." *Good Housekeeping*, November 2001, 108–113, 188.

Smith, Will. "Pop Quiz with Will Smith." *People*, April 1, 2002, volume 57, i12, 24.

Smolow, Jill, J. D. Reed, and Anne-Marie O'Neill. "Labor Days! With Their Men Standing By, Madonna, Catherine Zeta-Jones and Iman Give Birth to New Little Scene-Stealers." *People*, August 28, 2000, volume 54, i9, 58–55.

Spada, James. *Streisand, Her Life*. New York: Crown, 1995.

Stern, Isaac. *My First 79 Years*. New York: Knopf, 1999.

Tauber, Michael. "UpFront: Celine Dion." *People*, March 19, 2001, 54–58.

Thatcher, Margaret. *The Path to Power*. New York: HarperCollins, 1995.

The Oxford Annotated Bible. Edited by Herbert G. May and Bruce M. Metzger. New York: Oxford University Press, 1962.

Thomas, Dylan. *Selected Letters of Dylan Thomas*. Edited and with commentary by Constantine Fitzgibbon. London: Dent, 1966.

Thurman, Uma. *Rosie*, May 2001, 141–143.

Tracy, Kathleen. *Imus: America's Cowboy*. New York: Carroll & Graf, 1999.

Tylo, Hunter. *Making a Miracle*. New York: Pocket, 2000.

Ullmann, Liv. *Choices*. New York: Knopf, 1984.

Ustinov, Peter. *Dear Me*. Boston: Atlantic Monthly Press, 1977.

Vanderbilt, Gloria. *A Mother's Story*. New York: Knopf, 1996.

Wadia-Ells, Susan. (Editor). *The Adoption Reader: Birth Mothers, Adoptive Mothers, and Adopted Daughters Tell Their Stories*. Seattle: Seal Press, 1995.

Weinraub, Bernard, and Paula Chin. "Cindy's Family Focus." *Ladies Home Journal*, January 2002, 30–31, 99.

Wideman, John. "This Man Can Play." *Esquire*, May 1998, volume 129, number 5, 66–76.

Wiesel, Elie. *And the Sea Is Never Full: Memoirs 1969–* . Translated from the French by Marion Wiesel. New York: Knopf, 1999.

Winwar, Frances. *The Immortal Lovers: Elizabeth Barrett and Robert Browning, a Biography*. New York: Harper, 1950.

Wolf, Jeanne. "Oh, Boy." *Redbook*. March 1999, volume 192, i5, 86–83.

———. "Michelle Pfeiffer, What Lies Beneath." *Redbook*, August 2000, 93–95, 122.

———. "Let's Go." *Redbook*, November 2000, 124–128.

Woods, Vicki. "Cindy Crawford, California Cool." *Vogue*, August 2002, 222–225, 311–312.

SOURCES

Woolf, Virgina. *The Diary of Virginia Woolf, Volume II: 1912–1922*. Edited by Anne Olivier Bell. New York: Harcourt Brace Jovanovich, 1976.

Yeats, W. B. *The Letters of W. B. Yeats*. Edited by Alan Wade. New York: Macmillan, 1955.

Young, Andrew. *An Easy Burden, The Civil Rights Movement and the Transformation of America*. New York: HarperCollins, 1996.